FOOTPRINTS

Poetry
and threads of a poetical impression

RIFET BAHTIJARAGIC

Trafford
PUBLISHING™

Edited by: George Payerle

Cover Artwork by: Bill Hoopes
Painting: "Shoot to the Moon"

Translated from "The Bosnian" by: Sanja Garic - Komnenic,
Dennis Dehlic
Andrew Grundy

Note for Librarians: A cataloguing record for this book is available from Library and Archives Canada at www.collectionscanada.ca/amicus/index-e.html

Printed in Victoria, BC, Canada.

ISBN: 978-1-4251-7368-5

www.trafford.com

North America & international
toll-free: 1 888 232 4444 (USA & Canada)
phone: 250 383 6864 ♦ fax: 250 383 6804
email: info@trafford.com

The United Kingdom & Europe
phone: +44 (0)1865 722 113 ♦ local rate: 0845 230 9601
facsimile: +44 (0)1865 722 868 ♦ email: info.uk@trafford.com

10 9 8 7 6 5 4 3 2

CORPUS DELICTI

I apologize to my readers for potential
error, since this material hasn't
so far been scientifically finalized and argued
on the bases of empirical evidence. If somebody finds
any of my claims, spatial and temporal locations incorrect,
I will defend myself with the fact that the text in this book
belongs to the genre of literary fiction.
In my work, in addition to its poetic content,
there are possible imaginary connections with real roots
in the past of civilization. My purpose is to suggest
to contemporary and future generations
of the human species who the navigators of human happiness
could be. My intention is not to manipulate
the facts created in history
and in related fields which provide facts for history.
My intention is only to use the facts
in realizing the dream of human happiness.
Beings and occurrences in the book
are only the product of my imagination.

To Martin
from Rifel

OTHER BOOKS

By Rifet Bahtijaragic

Skice za cikluse (Sketches for Cycles), poetry, Sarajevo, former Yugoslavia, 1972

Urija (Barren), poetry, Belgrade, former Yugoslavia, 1982

Krv u ocima (Blood in the Eyes), novel, Wuppertal, Germany, 1996

Bosanski bumerang (Bosnian Boomerang), novel, Tuzla, Bosnia, 2001

Oci u hladnom nebu / Eyes to the Cold Sky, poetry, bilingual edition, Tuzla, Bosnia, 2004

Tragovi (Footprints), poetry and prose, Tuzla, Bosnia, 2008

TRANSLATOR'S COMMENTS

An attempt to recreate original forms in a foreign material is always inadequate. Words and ideas can never be perfectly matched and elucidated in translation. The unique melodies and rhythms of the original language are irreparably lost. However, Rifet Bahtijaragic's *Footprints* – a collection of poetry and prose deeply rooted in Bosnian soil and completed in Canadian multiculturalism – reaches far beyond the regional or the ethno-specific, making it readily accessible to the Canadian reader despite those shortcomings of translation. *Footprints* invites readers to look at themselves through the eyes of a foreigner, a foreigner who is equally at home in the realms of the universe and in his native Bosnia. Readers will look at themselves in these pages no matter where they are from, because these pages are about everyone, any human being. Rifet creates simple, graspable explanations for the secrets of the universe as well as for those of the human heart. His cosmic poetry and prose offer the hope that somewhere, beyond the world we have created, there are worlds we can communicate with and thus, maybe, be saved from ourselves.

—Sanja Garic-Komnenic

EDITOR'S COMMENTS

Rifet Bahtijaragic's Footprints leaves a deep impression on the human heart and mind. There is prose in the form of fictive interviews with a broad spectrum of leaders in our turbulent times – Marshal Tito, Michael Moore, the Dalai Lama, and Stephen Hawking. There is poetry born out of the recent Bosnian War – lyrical, bitter, impassioned, searching, and ultimately hopeful.

The book consists of three Parts – no titles for them, Parts of a journey. Suggestive, perhaps, of the unspeakable, but in fact emblematic of the unnameable. For this is a book of faith, not in a nameable god, but in the resilience of the human spirit, and its need for assistance from beyond.

First Part contains an interview with Marshal Tito which makes it perfectly clear that the crumbling of Yugoslavia into its warring constituent pieces need never have happened had there been a leader of Tito's stature to succeed him. Rifet rejects much of what Tito stood for, but accepts him as the sort of leader whose vision is capable of transcending factional interests and creating a viable, peaceable state. In Second Part, Bahtijaragic speaks with the Dalai Lama, and it's clear that here is another sort of leader who, if heeded, could lead the world toward peace. In Third Part, conversation with Stephen Hawking reveals the plausibility of looking to contact with extraterrestrials as a resolution to Earth's conflicts. While I've never rejected the possibility that UFO reports sometimes are valid, Rifet Bahtijaragic is the first writer on the subject I've encountered of whom I can't think he's just spinning a yarn. I might not believe in

UFOs yet, but I do believe in Rifet. These interviews are all fictitious, but compellingly believable.

In my view, the poetry in this book far surpasses the prose as literature. It is some of the finest poetry I've ever had the privilege to work with. But its excellence lends passionate and lyrical force to the prose, which makes explicit ideas and opinions we should all heed. It has been an honor to be asked to work with these translations of writing I believe to be, not only excellent, but important in a way that little writing is.

—George Payerle

CONTENTS

Third Part

Poetry

FOREWORD

Rifet Bahtijaragic, a Canadian and Bosnian writer, has for some time been broadening the cultural activities of Bosnians far away from Europe, in Canada. After the publication of his two novels, *Blood in the Eyes* and *Bosnian Boomerang,* came a collection of poetry, *Eyes in the Cold Sky.* Now he has given us *Footprints, Poetry and threads of a poetical impression.* In form and content it is a unique, innovative book. It comprises poetry and poetical/philosophical essayistic prose, which jointly interweave the personal and the regional, the general and the global, the national and the supra-national, the emotional and the philosophical, the earthly and the cosmic – all stemming from a human need to understand the essential questions of endurance and the survival of civilization.

The book *Footprints* induces memories of and comparisons with high achievements of human thought in the books *The Principals of a New Science,* by Giovanni Battista , *The Builders of the World,* by Stefan Zweig, and *Science and World,* by Ljubomir Berberovic. *Footprints,* with the richness of its themes, motives, and genres, is a unique and unusual spiritual laboratory, reaching for high achievements of human civilization and, in an artistic form, making them instrumental in the struggle for the betterment of humanity. Probably *Footprints* is thematically and, in terms of genre, most interesting since the poet in his artistic and philosophical lamentations has created fictitious, but factually very possible, interviews with important and inspiring people of our civilization.

In this book the poet puts himself face to face with Josip Broz, known to the world as Marshal Tito of Yugoslavia, and interviews him, asking very coldly analytical and almost merciless questions. The Marshal responds in kind, as was his way. From our perspective now, in 2008, the historical importance of the themes raised in this dramatic dialogue cannot be overstated. Also, those who had a chance to get to know him most authentically over long periods of time will be amazed by the originality and verisimilitude of the interview with Tito more than two and a half decades after the Marshal's physical death.

In the poet's youth, Tito and America were his hopes for the happiness of humanity, its liberation from incessant strife and misery. If in his mature years the hope was no longer Tito's vision of uniting the world, how can it *today* be the America of George Bush Jr., an America which has sunk from being the hope of humanity to becoming the generator of its fear? The poet turns to the Dalai Lama. Why? God is always alive as a metaphor, as a vividly expressed notion, as an allegory, as a reflection upon the reality of the material world, and as icon of the primordial human desire for the existence of the irrational in life. If it were possible for God to appear today – concretely, sensually, spiritually, transparently among people, then he would doubtless have the Dalai Lama's features. This holy man with the common touch, brought to Mount Gabel Musa on Sinai by the poet's imagination, voices the most noble, interesting, beautiful and healing thoughts to the human beings of today's civilization.

In the first part of this book, Rifet Bahtijaragic moves from hope to the weakening of belief in the efficacy of hope, from astonishment and puzzlement at man raising his arm against other men, to the scream and whisper that "God ordered Abraham, or Ibrahim, / To sacrifice a ram instead of a human. / God ordered!" Within the rejection of religious/ethnic conflict to be found throughout *Footprints,* this pairing of the Hebrew and Arabic names for the same prophet is significant.

In the second part of *Footprints,* the poet, through the power of his imagination, makes contact with the Dalai Lama and urges him to tell people how to become good. He recreates the Biblical and Kur'an scene of God telling the prophet the commandments for the creation of goodness in people. Then he starts to doubt whether people ever did follow in the past, do follow now or will yet follow the commandments of God, and he moves to the third part of this book.

In his imaginary meeting with Stephen Hawking, and in the context of the "Hawaii Declaration on Peaceful Relations with Extraterrestrial Civilizations," the poet spins threads for the rebirth of our civilization. Man is not only an earthly life form. He is part of the universe and a product of the laws of the universe. Rifet Bahtijaragic has already essayed voyages towards cosmic relations, especially in his novel *Bosnian Boomerang*. The poet employs an interview with the most prominent of today's savants in the science of the universe, Stephen Hawking, to seek proof of extraterrestrial civilizations. In the "Hawaii Declaration" he sees new hope that, in contact with much more intellectually advanced forms of life in the universe, people will finally learn that we on Earth are *all* human beings, and that each man should be responsible for the happiness of global humanity.

The traces Rifet Bahtijaragic illumines in this book go toward the past of civilization. Along this path "the threads of a poetical impression" find motives that amaze us and help us to see "how the world looks turned upside down" (Ellen Elias-Bursac). However, the traces in this book go toward the future as well. If on that path toward the unknown human beings do not follow the Dalai Lama's recommendations, there is yet hope that aliens, more intelligent and humane than we on the planet Earth, will give us their hand and save us.

—Milivoje Jeftic

POST SCRIPTUM

The poet's act of creation begins when his psyche, tired of meandering in everyday life, comes out through the perforated membrane of the mind and creates its own world, to which the reality of everyday life is only a gene that brings forth his inheritance. That process of creation happens under a veil not easily removed; it is difficult to discern its paths, the same as it would be difficult to engage the mind of an onlooker with all those processes happening under the surface of turbulent foaming water in the zone of some of the Icelandic geysers.

Immanent to poetry is an unusual way of the functioning of the human mind: an unordinary spectrum of its activities. Its ordinary activities are related to physical survival of the human body, movements, coordination, food supply, reproduction ... However, the poet's mind abandons the programmed routes of brain functioning. Electrical impulses do not move according to programmed schemes. They are liberated from the biological cords in the net, and they build new connections, grow wings, leave visible lines, and fly above ordinary routs. Poets do not "suffer" from the ordinary, planned, logical, and psychologically explainable ... They freely engage in new ways of creating relationships, mix time searching for the most appropriate one, build a specific architecture of space, take over a creative role, and determine the characteristics of their creations. In their job, reproduction is not genetic; it does not start from the genes in which solutions are embedded. For poets, genes are only life initiators whose aspects and relations depend on always-new forms of the functioning of their mind.

Different paths of thought creation originate from the fact that every human being, although belonging to the human species, has his own personalized mind. Certainly, there are no two painters who, given the same task, would paint the same paintings, nor are there two poets, composers ... Poetry is able to express a stance and a philosophical thought in an artistic form, with the images created by sounds evoking smells, with symbols and metaphors; it does it in a personal manner, always different, and is able, unlike exact sciences, to provoke the reader to participate in that creation and to model it according to his own possibilities.

The creation of all my poems was triggered by an event or by my dealings with the outside real world, or originated inside my imagination, sometimes logical, but often only instinctive and unnatural ... In all my poems that contact is enforced and terribly and deeply emotional. It does not mean that my poems would trigger the reader's mind in the same way, because each reader will discover her/his own personal input in his/her inner or outside world and will build upon it in his/her own way.

When I asked the Canadian poet George Bowering if he had been surprised by my words about his poetry, he replied that he had never seen himself as a poet who sees things in their perpetual movements, and that is how I see his poetry; I am equally positive that with the Bosnian poet Abdulah Sidran I would forever discuss my understandings of his poetry as an artistic way of expressing historical determinants refined in his mind.

Poetry is healing, aggressive, and ambitious. It is not satisfied with anything created in space and time. Not even with the ideas of the wise, the destructions of the ungracious, or with the contours of the beginning and the end in the theory of relativity. Regardless of its outer form, physiognomy, obvious goal and imagery, the poetic creation is a very wide and deep world that readers can see with their eyes, hear its sounds with their ears; however, they can discover it in a much more complex manner only with their mind. The poetic creation is not a framed picture. It is alive. It is the world in which time pulsates and spaces change. It can fulfill the everlasting, hushed human desire for eternity. A poem should be looked at from the outside, as a woman: looked at for a long time and with all senses, but only as long as it takes the reader to find on its surface the passages into the world for which the poem is an opening to an ever new and rich life. A poem usually has many such opening and all depends on readers (travelers, researchers) and on what way they discover it and through which one they squeeze into that world. It also depends on through which passage they enter into the poet's mind and feelings, and how courageously and skillfully they travel that mind and those feelings, through always-new times, spaces, and relations. That journey does not have an end because the poet's mind is only one of the passages into the richness of the worlds touched by the poet, no matter whether he traveled the roads of reality or of imagination.

The opening on the outer form of the poem can be no more than one word (*stećak* – a medieval Bosnian tomb-stone) or a poetic image (*or as when in the heart of a harbor / in the sails of sleeping vessels / a sudden wave brings about / thirst for running / dance on water*), or a sound (*in the mystical sound of brass, the past awakens me*), a smell (*this morning the smells in cafés awakened*), a feeling (*words feel miserable*), or only one recorded ticking of time ... Sometimes the poet's world is so hermetical that the reader needs an extraordinary amount of energy to pass through the current of life which one writing in that world pours into his poem. Almost the same amount of energy would be needed to pass through a black hole in the galaxy against its enormous gravitational force, and continue a voyage across the rich world of the universe. While one analyzes a poem, it is enough to discover only one of the convenient passages into the poet's mind and then move within it in a desired manner and as far as an individual reader needs.

That much I think about the writing of poetry. Whatever you find in my poems, it will have been made in this way, as coal and oil have been made by the Earth's heat and pressure, and perhaps as the fire in the heart of the sun has been made by cosmic fusion.

First Part

MAN IS THE MEASURE OF ALL THINGS

I AM NOT SURE WHAT happened first: Greek democracy or Protagoras. I would not say that it does not matter. I am more likely to assume that with the Greek statesmen the conditions for the birth of democracy were ripening, and then Protagoras came with his proverb *Man is the measure of all things.* He only philosophically shaped into a proverb the intention of the society of that time. And then the proverb was accepted by sophists, the ideologists of the slave-owning democracy, who went through towns and villages teaching people the simple ideology that places people on the pedestal of all values. Two and a half millennia from then, nowadays, the sophists do not tread the roads of our world. Above man we put profit, the bleakest cause of the exploitation of man and the satanic child of the greatest machinations. Instead of the slave-owing democracy of Protagoras' time, we have imperialistic democracy ruling the societies of our civilization. The former had a lot inhumanity in itself and was only for free people, but the latter is not much better. However, the former is twenty five centuries old; ours warns that we have not much moved from the beginning.

To me democracy has always been peace and flocks of white

doves soaring above stadiums and the world's harbors. Maybe my sight has been cloned, so I do not see anymore as a common human being would; instead of white doves flying from one part of the Earth to another with the messages of peace, I more and more see black warships lining the world's harbors.

I was born in the first year of peace after World War II. As soon as I was able to understand what war among people means, I wondered why people go to war. Why does someone fight who could achieve divine values in peace? As soon as I became aware of the danger that is the destiny of human society, my spirit held tightly onto that which gave me hope. Tito became the symbol of my hope in the country where they bore me without asking where I wanted to be born. And in that big mysterious world beyond the border of my country, my hope became America, from the moment when we at our homes started having flour, dry cod, butter, cheese, powdered eggs … from generous Truman's help; and when our teacher Maria in the second grade of the elementary school explained that the pillars of all people's happiness were America and Russia.

The world was showing itself to me as fast as time was passing. I was happy, though more hungry than fed, because my imagination was carrying me into the time of peace and prosperity. I dreamed of how I would build a nice house and how I would be opening its gate from the distance of a hundred meters, without meddling with alchemy and without somebody burning and destroying it in my life-time. And I dreamed of how I would travel around the world: one month to be a Japanese, the other a Swede or a Canadian, Russian, Congolese … And I wrote poems about people and nature. And then life started becoming corrupted. My first confusion happened when one night my mother told me that her father and my grandfather, Medan Medic, had been killed by Tito's partisans in 1942, in Bihac, in Bosnia, because he had been a forest ranger and would punish some partisans for illegally pillaging the forest. Then I was astonished when in grade seven a history teacher nicknamed Shampoleon , without any fear in his voice, explained that in the history of the world the greatest crime in the smallest unit of time had been the American attack on Hiroshima and Nagasaki with atomic bombs.

The greatest number of people were killed in the shortest period of time since the beginning of all wars. The killing of innocent men, women, children, the old, the disabled ... For that reason my two great hopes became less great and encircled with doubt.

I am not any longer at the age when my human spirit can be satisfied with hope. Maybe I have matured more then I should. I am also above cursing those who brought me the evil, and who continue to bring evil to humanity. I do not believe in the time of punishment. I have always loved life and looked for ways to catch all opportunities waiting for me. I believe that it is every person's need and that everybody's intellect drives humanity to look for happiness. That is why I have decided to square accounts with my two hopes and try to find out if I was too hasty in my rejection.

Tito was not easy to find. After his death, the Yugoslavian people drowned him in a sea of tears, and every person at his funeral took a part of that famous man. It was not easy for me. There was need to unify the millions of Tito's particles, which Yugoslavians had carried with them, swearing they were all Tito; and also to unify those particles that the representatives of 123 other nations had carried home to their countries. Among them were 32 presidents, 22 prime ministers, 4 kings – participants at the most famous funeral in the history of our civilization. I even stole something of Tito from Mrs. Lillian, the mother of then-president of the United States, Jimmy Carter, who had sent her as his representative to Tito's funeral. Having done all this, I attacked Tito right away, provoking him openly, as if one's mother has left him, and when he finds her, he starts tearing at her clothes:

You succeeded in becoming an idol and in moving the masses to follow you, ordering them to do what you wanted them to do because you were the master of music before today's showbiz musicians were. You did the same as they do at the onset of the third millennium: move the masses at stadiums, plazas and halls, ordering the audience to sing the arias from their albums. And then in the masses' ovations all those ugly things that could be attributed to a human being disappear, for human society is destined to march following leaders. It is easier to justify the marching if masses follow the one who was the last of the great men from World War II, the one who prevailed in Hitler's and Stalin's attacks, the one who, during the animosities of the Cold War, was building bridges of friendship among nations, who was one of the founders of the Movement of Nonaligned Nations, dulling the blades of the two powerful, confronted blocks in the world of that time. Even when they, as Fitzroy MacLean wrote, follow one who is energetic, adroit, decisive, tireless; who is not an ascetic, fanatic ideologist nor a bureaucratic dogmatist, but one who is a hedonist, the boss not the subordinate; one who is extremely broad minded, with a sense of humor and open affection for small things, possessing natural shyness, a female temperament in bursts of anger, consideration and nobility. In reality, you were not a communist. Instead you played in the political life as in film. I do not blame you because masses followed you blindly. It is not your drawback but only the basic characteristic of masses. Customs and ideas are the work of an infinitesimally small minority of people, while masses are always similar in their ignorance, ready to accept everything, even lies, cruel when they have a chance, selfish and narrow-minded. They forgive you for the crimes of your freedom fighters, merciless killing and persecution of Chetniks, Ljotics, Ustashas, and of your other enemies who refused to surrender. Then, Goli Island, a cruel prison for your collaborators who stayed faithful to Stalin.

T I T O: It is easy to be smart when time shows you what is smart! It is easy to mock my mistakes and the falls I took while I was walking through a thicket full of holes and traps, and you are sitting on a hill and looking at my failures. It is easy to blame me for broken branches in the thicket through which I was rushing. I was not Mahatma Gandhi during the first phase of the path along which I was leading the Yugoslavian people. I said *"Better the graveyard than slavery"* because the latter meant collaboration with the blackest ideology of the world. Not because I liked war. I have always been against war. Our crimes at the end of the war? By that rule, every court that condemns a criminal would also be criminal. What do you think, how many enemies, and many more innocent people, the Americans, British, and Russians killed while liberating Europe from the Nazis and Fascists?

With regard to Goli Island, it was my fault. We were precipitate in solving the problem we faced after refusing Stalin's baton, and we tried to isolate all those who had not understood the meaning of our "NO". We did not have Siberia, nor were we at such a level of democracy that we could neutralize interior enemies who could easily have triggered a civil war and enabled a Soviet intervention. Goli Island was similar to the present American use of Guantanamo Bay, but it very quickly stopped being a prison because I understood it was our historical minus.

Communist? I first heard that idea from our village priest, and I was drawn to it during the very dark time of the twentieth century when inhumane, nationalistic regimes were spreading death around the world. Stalin and his satellites, Chinese leaders, and even some well known Western politicians and philosophers took away from me my attribute of *"communist"*.

You left sharp blades in the relationships among the Yugoslavian nations, who spilt blood after you were gone, and you did not revise religions in a manner that would forever give people pause in their relations with God and prevent them from placing religion above all other human relationships.

T I T O: If a swarm of bees fell into your lap, it would be hard for you to turn them into insects without dangerous stingers. It takes a long time to affect their behavior because nation and religion are imbedded deep in human genes. They have existed for thousands of years. They are almost instinctive reactions of the human spirit. I encouraged love among people, their mixing in order to dull the blades of nationalism and religion. I advocated equality and brotherhood where one's nationality would be only a statistic, rather than a motivation for mobilizations. It is the same with religious institutions. A motivation for people should be their spiritual and economic progress.

Your maxims on relations among people live after your death. Nowadays, the Dalai Lama, Desmond Tutu and others are using them. The maxim "Guard brotherhood and unity like the apple of *your eye", addressed to the part of civilization where you ruled, is not new. It has been known in history. Mahatma Gandhi spoke in a similar manner. Winston Churchill stumbled upon it too. Many rulers preached the unity of their people. You did it very successfully. In the structure of your state mechanism, besides the fatherly treatment, it was not difficult to find dictatorship and force, as well as serious and severe consequences if one dared to have a different opinion. It is hard to judge whether you, with the help of the maxim, ruled over the Yugoslavian people and their religions, or whether you forced that idea into the brains of your followers in order to control them more easily. Maybe you did not really care if it was hypocrisy and how much of it would go into the genes of the future generations. But I like your idea because it helps the survival of the whole as well as of the qualitative differences. It is the escape from unitarization. Similar is the Canadian concept of multiculturalism and especially the concept of the creation of United Europe.*

T I T O: What would happen if all the flowers in a field had the same color? Or the same shape? To say the least, insects would be confused. There have been attempts to forget our historical quarrels through unitarization. But it is wrong. Why should we all have the same name? It is important that a different name does not bother anybody. It is important to build different values in life. It is important that our first concern be man, every human being and their happiness. My idea of the path for the future was not to allow the diversification of interests, and not to favor the general over the personal, but to globalize and at the same time preserve national values that are everybody's values. To enable and force crossbreeding, by combining what is good in one identity with what is good in another and prevent incestuous degenerations. To combine the smart and the economically potent in order to become competitive in the world. So, united and powerful, we were not afraid of seeking other possibilities for unification in the world, in the world's division of labor. In that case you do not feel like a minority, you are not afraid that the others will swallow you. You can open borders and mix with others because your contribution in the world's genetics will be indestructible.

And dictatorship? In the world, they call you a humane dictator. A dictator is a dictator. Your election system was guided and limited.

T I T O: You can not force truths upon history. I was a sort of dictator, but at the time when it was needed. Don't young fruit trees need strong support in the form of wooden sticks firmly put in the ground to protect the trees from strong winds?! Especially when a wind has the intention to destroy them. Later we democratized the way we thought was good. Gradually. Isn't the concept of self-governed socialism an exceptional form of democracy? It is not my fault that people saw me as the father of the nation and gave me the eternal throne, or better a sofa, on some hill from where I can see them all. But they can see me, too. As far as I know, they wanted me to be with them forever.

Another maxim of yours was accepted by many all over the world: "The peoples of the world need to build their relationships on the principles of peaceful coexistence." You and your friends Nehru and Nasser based your Movement of Nonaligned Nations on that principle. I believe you had in mind the protection of the weaker from the stronger and the more aggressive. In the world's social and economic processes, you wanted to ensure the confrontation of different ideas and to enable a spontaneous competition, and to leave it to the spectators to choose their favorites. However, isn't it at the same time giving a hand to those who exploit and suppress others? For peaceful coexistence knows all forms of state apparatus and types of government. And some kind of closed borders. Does it mean that internationalization, which means putting pressure on evil governments, would only stay at the level of verbal confrontation of ideas and philosophies? Would it mean freezing of the state of affairs in the world and choosing the path that would, in the third millennium, enable the domination of strict borders and god-given systems, regardless of what is within these borders? Is it the demand that everybody do his own business, his family affairs, without any regard for what is happening in other houses? Or does it mean that today Bush's Administration in America needs to be prevented from destroying and conquering other regions and people, under the pretext of enforcing democracy? Or that we should wait indefinitely until, in the countries governed by evil governments, the time ripens when positive forces will be able to destroy their own evil? What is AB OVO? If an egg did not have fertilizer, would life be possible? Have you ever thought that coexistence could simply be tolerance and that it could stop the cloning of life in the third millennium?

T I T O: Hadrian did not accept Christianity because he preferred the diversity of life with different gods that were similar to humans. The domination of one is a dogma, especially when that dominance is enforced from the outside, and even worse, by war, killings, and destruction. Those are paths creating hatred. People should respect and help each other so they can live more easily and rely on one another. One's dignity should mean a lot to others. Peaceful coexistence is an extraordinary recipe for uniting humanity. It is the only way for people to stop thinking about war, regardless if it is a war to conquer or defend. One whose doctrine is war arms oneself, and no weapon in history has ever been left unused. It has always been used against people. Peaceful coexistence offers us love, mutual respect and freedom from interference. When you get rid of hatred, you will get rid of the basic problems that make people confront each other: religion, nation, race ... It is an extraordinary recipe for the honorable integration of the world. Wars will never integrate the world because they encourage destructive instincts, both in victims and in predators.

It is believed that the processes of transformation of the communist systems started with Gorbachev. It seems to me, and I am almost positive, that they started with your successful, patient, and gradual revisionism, which materially and politically supported the West in its open conflict with communism, and also the East in its slow advance toward prosperity, with an ever greater gap between party bureaucracy and mass of the people. Because of its rapid industrial development, the opening of its borders toward the world, and happier and freer lives of its people after the 1960s, your Yugoslavia became the love of its own people, and in Eastern European countries it was called America. "Yugoslavian syndrome" became the obsession of many countries and peoples in the world because it prevailed under the pressure of big powers. The past outrage in the communist countries at your revisionism turned into a more and more heated urge for opening their borders toward the world and the democratization of their political and economic conditions.

T I T O: At first we were stubborn and self-confident, and later world affairs played into our hands, supporting our endeavor to prosper quickly in peace and freedom. Squeezed between the orthodox-communist East and the capitalist West, we were taking good recipes from both and wove them into our concept of self-governed socialism. People fell in love with us during the revolution, and their love was strengthened as workers were given greater rights. Self-governed socialism was a system that placed people above all other values, labor above profit - which was even the doctrine of some great Americans such as Abraham Lincoln and Thomas Jefferson. I am fond of most of the philosophy called "communist doctrine". However, I have never been slave to anything except the desire to help people to live happily. I was not slave to the communist doctrine, but I have always thought that profit keeps the true riches of civilization – *humanity and freedom* – behind bars. Profit is the deception of people, a black force that destroys morality and dignity. For the sake of profit, Bush's America wants to enslave the world. For its sake Princess Diana cannot rest in peace. For its sake, super-developed societies destroy the concept of family, one of the strongest human institutions ever, so that teenagers can sooner start working for meager pay, caught in the claws of profiteers. Then I realized that this process is an unstoppable force implanted in human genes, along with egoism, but that it is possible to humanize the ways people make profit, making it available for all. The problem with communist systems lay in their narrow-mindedness, in hatred of any revisionism, as if changes were not the power engine of all societies.

I had prepared a few more questions, but Tito had vanished. He disappeared in the mass of former Titoists, who destroyed his work and brought evil upon those he had loved. I mostly regretted that I had not criticized him more directly for having been devoted to the unity of nations but, at the same time, not having tried as devotedly to eliminate the divisions along nationalist lines in his own country. Also, I regretted not having asked if he really believed that people could accept the philosophy of peaceful coexistence and eliminate the human thirst for profit and fanatic terror.

When Tito died in 1980, my friends in France told me that it is pity that Tito was a Yugoslavian because Yugoslavians would soon completely bury him. If he had been French, they said, he would have been bigger then Napoleon. And I was angry. I told them he was ours, but, at the same time, he was guilty of the murder of my grandfather, as my mother had told me at bedtime when I was young. And that is a big minus for him in my feelings.

And America?! America is my big sorrow. Faith in its goodness weaned me of the communist ideology, attracted me to the American continent, and then hurled me face-first into the realization that I am naïve and silly like most idealists. To secure survival one needs to be stronger and bigger than others – if not by peaceful means, then by force. Clinton was my last American spring, a charming leader possessing human values, like the Roman imperator Hadrian. When he had to relinquish power, I cursed the system of mandates, which shortens the times when good leaders sow happiness and enables their successors to be even the blind and mentally ill. The media's and politicians' desire to guillotine him because of an affair with a young woman gave me a warning that such a democracy looks very much like a church's dogma. Clinton's case shook America as a distant earthquake, but after the earthquake came a destructive tsunami in the shape of Clinton's successor, George W. Bush. This president reminded me of a magnificent star turned into a white dwarf in the universe, which can grow only in creating a destructive explosion. He led America into a war against humanity, institutionally proclaimed that the war is a sacred affair of every American patriot, and on the title page engraved a bleeding cross, not unlike a swastika, far from my faith in goodness and God.

I wanted to talk to Bush, but I was afraid of him and, instead, decided to talk to Michael Moore in order to test if I was right in losing my second hope for the happiness of humanity and to justify my attempts to find hope beyond the limits of our Mother Earth.

I met Michael on Granville Island in Vancouver. He was standing ten meters away from a poster for his movie *Fahrenheit 9/11* and was jotting down the passersby's reactions. It seemed to me he could not wait for somebody to recognize him and start talking to him.

What is closer to truth, I started our conversation , *my idea that democracy will bring about America's fall or your thought that America will make democracy ashamed? Or, maybe, simpler, is democracy one of the inevitable postulates on the path to human happiness? Moore was looking somewhere above my head as he replied.*

M O O R E: The word *democracy,* meaning political and social relationships among people, is always the same. However, every case of democracy is specific. Democracy is not always positive. Not unlike tyranny, democracy can also be a choice for evil because the evil is often attractive, smooth-tongued, dishonest and full of empty promises. Democracy should depend on the intellectual conscience of people, but it depends mostly on the socio-economic conditions of those participating in democracy. For example, George W. Bush was elected the president of the United States for the second time by cheating the nation, bribing the greedy, and telling lies to the gullible. And by persuading half of the nation that, without him, each one of them would have a terrorist behind his back. Only he is capable of spreading the fear of terrorism worldwide. However, he did not tell his people the truth that he and his gang instigate hatred of America in the world and make the number of terrorists multiply, especially by committing crimes against the Iraqi people.

I believe these are crimes against the American people, against our entire civilization, I added.

M O O R E: We are used to being respected in the world, and people do not have enough information on how quickly we are sinking. America had a great role in the Second World War, with the exception of the dropping of the atomic bombs, but in all the successive wars, its role was disputable. Recently, looking historically, America has started wars in the world under the pretext of fighting the communist tyranny, then of establishing democracy and freedom for people, and finally of fighting terrorism and its helpers. Why? Because all wars became the means of creating profit, not for the American people but for the owners of American capital, which thrives on the unhappiness of others. Bush is only a marionette of that intent and a despicable liar. In Cambodia, Congo, Brazil, Indonesia, the Middle East … America helped tyrants to gain power, but preached the battle for democracy. These tyrants succeeded with American help and destroyed people mercilessly. Those who make decisions about America's war moves are not concerned about liberating people from oppressive regimes. No, they also talk about their concern for our security, but, in fact, they are more concerned about their own interests.

Bush's Administration has several times changed its reasons for going to war in Iraq.

M O O R E: We all know that. They did not try to deceive their people by playing a smart intellectual game. They used poor lies, covertly provoked protests in the world community and brought a terrible disaster upon the Iraqi people. Iraqi people, instead of wholeheartedly greeting American liberation from Saddam's tyranny, very soon wished Saddam were back. When Iraqis were asked if they wanted the inauguration of American-style democracy, the polls showed that they massively cried against democracy, and begged the Americans to reestablish tyranny or fundamentalism. Why? Because even Iraqi children know that the Americans did not come to establish well-being but to occupy their oil-rich country and to establish their power in that part of the world. Bush managed to sentence Saddam to death, but who is going to sentence to death an even bigger criminal, Bush Junior?

The fear of America's power is growing in the world.

M O O R E: We are talking about dominance in the world. For that purpose, Americans under this Administration will go and occupy any part of the world, if that is in their interest. They will even block science and scientific truths and achievements in order to longer exploit what brings them profit. For example, they say the hydrogen fueled engine is a nonsense because of its production cost, but they fail to tell people that such a fuel will save the resources for life on Earth, and that, by relying on oil, which will be exhausted by 2015, humanity will face a catastrophe. I can imagine what America will do to prevent Brazil from starting massive production of the hydrogen based fuel.

I was naïve. When Orwell's book 1984 was published, I thought it could apply to anything but America.

M O O R E: It applies to America most. The America directed by Bush II. He convinces the American people that the threat of terrorism is so great that one would imagine millions of terrorists pointing their weapons at us. If that is his opinion, why doesn't he objectively explain to his people why terrorists target America above all? He convinces people that anti-American terrorism is not a temporary state of affairs but an eternal threat. Isn't that Orwell? The instigation of fear among people produces aggression, or, I may well say, it gives legitimacy to war machinery and war profiteers to attack wherever they estimate there is economic interest, regardless of the consequences for the people who are under attack or for Americans. In whose hands are we, O great American democracy, the land of great minds, artists and philanthropes?!

When people sense a real danger, it is natural that they react instinctively in defense. When they are drawn into irrational fear, a terrible murderer is created. This prompts us to hide guns under our pillows, to refuse to live beside people of different races or ethnicities or beside any foreigner. This is the best way to take from us our 200 years of freedom and to have the American people fall into the hands of the instigator of the "terrorist threat". Poor Statue of Liberty at the entrance to New York Harbor. They want to endlessly manipulate us with fear. They are worse than any exploiter ever. They took God into their own hands, and now they want to take eternal time into their hands too.

I, myself, am very scared. Isn't that, God forbid, proof that Karl Marx and Friedrich Engels were correct when they said that capitalism will enter the last stage of the development of human society, imperialism, after which comes the agony and cataclysm? It will happen only because capitalists will invest more in technology and less in workers. Are we going to face the sort of deluge described in the Kur'an and the Bible?

M O O R E: I am thinking about how we Americans have so easily accepted that game Bush II plays. What's happened to our intellect? We have also accepted the demagogy that we are far more powerful than others, and that we are the masters of the world. Number one in the world. I am positive that the average American does not want to dominate anybody. Then they invented fear. To scare the hell out of us, they need a big enemy. It is not the Soviet Union anymore. The extreme right-wing ideologists and politicians Wolfowitz, Rumsfeld, Kristal and Perle pushed a weakling, Bush II, into the fire. They invented the eternal war against terror. It is a very dangerous war doctrine for the entire world. In that manner, they create an eternal means for creating profit. How many of our lives and the lives of our children are they prepared to sacrifice for their interests? We are not going to get killed by terrorists but by our leaders and unscrupulous profiteers. We are almost at the stage when capitalists possess everything in the world, and all others are their slaves. Capitalists even now possess almost all land, houses, factories and money. And today, if somebody confronts them, they throw him in jail or take his job from him, letting him die of starvation. Instead, we, who are economically at the top of the world's civilization, should ensure that all people in the world have their basic needs met and can realistically dream of a better life. Instead of terrible destruction, fear, and absolute exploitation, we should have offered the world the solution for the drinking-water problem for all, enough water for all, and enough health care and medications for all – instead of paying the shameful 24 cents an hour for manufacturing our NBA uniforms in El Salvador, or 12 cents an hour to the Chinese for making cute Disney toys. Instead, we keep quiet while pregnant workers in Bangladesh are being beaten for making mistakes when sewing Gap clothes.

Bush II was elected again. He was elected even though he does not comply with the United Nations resolutions and disregards the Geneva Convention and the Hague Tribunal, and even though many great people in the world declare him a war criminal and demand his punishment. Some female musicians from Texas travel the world singing that they are ashamed of the fact that Bush is a Texan. Hollywood actors, writers, scientists, priests have raised their voices against him, yet he is elected again. It seems as if Al Capone's Chicago mafia has moved to the world's political and social scene.

M O O R E: I am not surprised. Nor even disappointed. Bush II did not surprise me by manifesting the victory of belligerent radicalism in the world's politics at the onset of the third millennium. He has already put America on a pedestal as the most hated country on our planet now. The world now is more afraid of America, which was its hope in the past, than it is afraid of communism or any tyranny. How about people? People have always been unpredictable. Most people think solely about their own interest, whatever that is, or they swim down the current that gets hold of them or that promises golden fields or other lies. I wake up at night scared of the question: Where is my country? I am positive that millions of Americans are asking themselves the same question. And American capital with Bush as leader reforms affairs on Earth using the Machiavellian principle that: In politics all means are allowed that help to conquer, then establish and spread the utmost power.

How about civilization?

In front of the poster for Moore's movie, a bunch of teenagers gathered, eagerly commenting on the photograph in which Michael Moore holds a statue of Bush II and is about to throw it into the abyss, in the same way people have thrown the statues of Hitler, Stalin, Ceausescu, Saddam Hussein ... Moore joined the group and started dancing to the rhythm of the music coming from the restaurant called Bridges. The teenagers began dancing too, then the passersby, and soon the entire crowd on Vancouver's Granville Island. Even the bakers came out of their bakeries, the waiters and chefs from the restaurants, the merchants from the stores ... They were all dancing. For me, it was the proof that people will outlive Bush II and his wars around the world, and that life is unstoppable. I was also dancing, and, following the rhythm of the music, I was coming closer to the spot where Moore was dancing in a trance. I managed to hear him telling those gathered around him that a new David was needed to gain victory over Goliath.

I do not think that Bush II imposed himself on Americans. In that powerful country, the conditions for the arrival of a radical president had already been created. The people were ready for such a government. Today in America, tomorrow ... Bush II is an artist in manipulating people. He and his big capitalists, not only in the President's party but also in the Democratic Party, and in other political movements, have invented a game to divide the poor and middle-class masses, making one half affiliate themselves with the elephants, and the other half with the donkeys so that they confront each other. While the people's masses fight with each other over politics, big capitalists from both sides fulfill their profit-making plans. I worry that others in the world might start emulating Bush II's recipe, in the same manner as Hollywood, Coca Cola, McDonald's ...

At the onset of the third millennium America finds itself in the position of a superpower without deep roots and without a strong gravitation capable of balancing the centrifugal forces at play in the world, and of grounding America in the spheres useful for civilization. There has been the same problem with all destroyers in the world's history. America's centrifugal forces are dangerous because, with their growth, the balance gets weaker, and the centripetal forces of that society are not capable of holding the balance with those forces that hasten out into the world and destroy all that is weaker. Doesn't the speed of America's means of transportation pose the threat of overpowering the force of gravitation and of separating itself from the Earth? Doesn't its computer technology threaten to put itself above the human mind and to drag all, including man, into the places of no return? Doesn't its war machinery threaten to take away the keys of peace and democracy and to enforce the autocracy and tyranny of murderous machines? Isn't the absurd dictatorial institution of the President, who can start a war without anything to stop him, already placed on top of America's democracy? Who can today believe in an electoral machinery which can, by the rule of insane inertia, elect an idiot, a moron, as the leader of the people's masses?

That is not all. For decades I have been looking for a way to comfort myself, to find any kind of hope for the salvation of civilization. When I observe good people, I become an optimist and I write verses full of the sun and fragrances. When I observe those others, I sink, and then lift my head toward the sky, looking for someone who could help us. People are not only bloodthirsty. They are also intelligent, but very egoistic, merciless, revengeful, and unforgiving ... Now the Serbs, because they lived for centuries under the Turkish Empire, have revenged themselves on the Bosnians. Serbs have been free for more than a hundred years. The Turkish Empire has become history. They revenged themselves on Bosnians for the misery they had endured, because as Muslims the Bosnians reminded them of Turks, and not of their brothers, Slavs. Perhaps those people who are today under the heel of Americans will one day revenge themselves on the future Americans. A crime once committed triggers a chain of crimes. Didn't it start with Cain and Abel? The brother killed his brother out of pride and egoism. Then the Abels revenge themselves on Cains, then Cains on Abels. And so on forever, people have been killing each other. What powerful artistry did that creator-genius need to create man from infinitesimal and formless cells and molecules and to make him biologically and mentally so complex and so incapable of achieving peace?!

That is why I advocate cloning, but I would first give that right to extraterrestrials, provided I had firm proof that in their own civilization they do not kill each other. I would allow them to clone our future generations and to create beings who know of no hate or aggression.

While I was writing the verses of the poem "The Sun", CNN was reporting that Americans, in the three years of the war in Iraq, had caused the death of more than 650 thousand Iraqis. In the next report, some Terry Smith from southern Texas was showing his horses to the reporters and explaining what he feeds them so that they win the race. *Diet is the future of the world,* he was saying, demonstrating a special horse diet. *This is a diet against everything that prevents them from winning the race!*

WAR

How could you say people deserve war!
Where did you get such a grotesque idea?!

Even when it is holy,
War destroys;
Humanity's everlasting wound.
The truths about the enemy
Are being invented.
War follows a cholera in the mind,
Wrapped in the deceiving cloak of profit.
Human hands crush
The blossoming scents of spring.

In glasses of filthy rapture
The ashes become laurels,
Bloodstained badges
The symbols
In carriages of doubtful pride.

Spring birds arrive on the wings of hope.
Instead of nests
Ashes
And moaning streams.
A frozen mystery at the root.

If winners write history,
The truth is not true.

In war,
Happiness is the unhappiness
Of others.

TOMBSTONE

and this tombstone
like a gemstone
witnesses
the forlorn time
of old defiance and rage

the tombstone here
and the one nearby
make our eyes see
that we did not fall from the skies
that in this cloven land
lies the root
which makes us all kin

and the tombstone
in the tempest of time
murmurs
that something deep inside
us
and you
consoles

and man is born
from something
like a drop of water in the sea

IF I WERE THE WIND

Were I the wind to winnow far and wide,
Along lanes and over meadows,
Through woods and groves,
Into blooming flowers …

Perhaps I would find you,
My sturdy children,
In some magic peaceable place.

Were I the wind to herd the traveling clouds,
Or follow the sun's golden rays,
Like a sprouting seed,
Like a questing doubt …

Perhaps I would recognize you
By your swaying hair
In the eyes of the nymphs.

Were I the wind to shimmer
Through the murmur of fountains,
And slide down the quaver of violins
Into the primal place where
Impulse awakens desire
To plumb the world's beginnings…

Perhaps I would take you up, my children,
On the rainbow's shoulders

To the hushed Eternal.

Were I the wind to melt the ice
From glacial mountains,
To bring forth mighty fire from the depths,
And the fateful old curse ...

I would raise you to the stars,
To some other, farther realm,
O, my bound desire!

February, 1994

INHERITANCE

I rode the grey horse down the fields,
And the many-colored tapestry on my chest
Unfurled to the sky.
I rode the grey horse with the wind,
And the white mane exploded,
Like a desert shattered in the purple light.

The southern wind passed through my fields,
And the sun gave them buds;
The flock from behind the mountain,
Across the mist,
Before our eyes,
Flew in as a red scarf.

They are gone,
Then return
From cradle to cradle …
Retreat!

The grasses sprouted on my fields
Now grow with yellowish boiling wolf's milk.
The birch and walnut trees are budding …
Returning from a long journey
Everything bursts into last year's love.

I rode the grey horse in the morning.
His chest began to foam,

And the road reached all the way to defiance.
I rode the grey horse at dusk,
And the hot sphere of the sun
Began inflating before my eyes,
And pulled out the quaking from my chest
As we rode downstream.

ENIGMA

I do not know how we came to be.
Old-time tales seem too mystical.
(Everyone takes wheat to his own granary!)
I do not even know when we parted,
Because the libraries of our Babel overflow
With volumes wrapped in bloody rags.

I simply no longer believe
The old truths and the new lies!

They told me a Thousand and One Nights
Of brotherhood and common blood
Of our grandfathers butchering one another.
Convincing me, and all others like me,
By scheme and by passion,
That our genes were the same!
… Even the ones known to be butchers.
That our genes were the same!

Sometimes I just wanted to dream
Of some creator in an old castle,
Some prophet …

I still do not know, when downriver,
Instead of clear waters and scented grasses,
Blood flows and stench spreads,
Who I am. Where I am from.

... And why all over again?

What kind of men use their brothers' skulls
To build the walls of their future?!
To whom will they tell new tales tomorrow?

THE PAST

The past creeps up in a ballet of sobs,
In a shrewish madness.
In its sunset, disturbances can be read,
The roots of shining medals
Tearful worlds.

In the past, each gram of progress
Swam in a sea of human tears.
Where love and hate were but two shoulders
Holding the head of the future.

Some asked the mathematician Nash
About his Nobel Prize,
While others were interested in his
Homosexual experiences.
Only Russell Crowe pleaded through tears
For them all to leave the man to his
Mystical genius.
The Laureate answered by mysteriously turning in his
Stormy geometrical circle.

If the past could return to the past,
And the future gave birth to the future,
If continuity could begin from nothing,
Ill-fated disturbances would remain
Twirling at their conception.

TIME

Time a spark beyond the eye's reach,
And a tremor whistling beyond our senses,
And a glass emptied of wine
Before the glass-blowers cheeks have glowed;
The wind
Discerned in the collision of temperatures.

Time is a picture torn from thoughts,
And the frozen tip of an Inuit boy's nose.
Spaces develop in time
And red volcanic lava darkens.
In time are borne the symbols of the past
And the present was imagined in minds long lost.

Just as you think you have hold of it,
That you have crawled your way
Into its immaterial structure
And that you have it,
That you have nailed it into Einstein's relativity,
It scatters itself with your ashes
And rings like the bells of the foggy distance.

Time meant precision to Kant,
To Tito, it was the magic of history,
To Clinton – the bitterness that follows pleasure,
To Sartre – infinity.

Time, in the defiled eyes of a Bosnian girl,
Has frozen into a surprise, a pearly shell of hope.

It is the butterfly's larva,
The fog's tadpole.
In time Goya's *Nude Maya*
Was racing around the windmills,
Wrapped in a cape of tulips.

Time is born in time
Paraphrased in calamity
Like a genie from a magic lamp
It gets free.

HUMAN

Politics are still playing with human lives!

Human is not just a word,
And human lives not just a simple phrase!

Human is more than feeling in a poem
And far beyond the complex hero of a novel.
Human is the creator of songs
And miraculous creations.

In the human imagination, life is ethereal,
And death sometimes the beginning of a new life,
And the faces of the gods remarkably similar to those
Of humans,
And the nature of Satan,
And the innocent, fearful eyes of fawns ...

Human is not a tombstone
With a pedigree in the album of life,
Nor some marginal branch on the family tree,
A picture in the frame of rainbow colors,
Runner, sailor, seducer, scoundrel ...

Human is an imagination from some other world,
A stylized pirouette in a boiling cosmos,
An image bursting with life.

Human is a Bosnian
Walking along Vancouver's Broadway
Breaking the chains of the silent past,
And peeking a look into the uncertain tomorrow,
Into mornings full of hope and protest induced by fear.

Human is a glance pregnant with thought,
And the breath of life fascinated by time
On the path into the unknown.

TEAR

The spark from the trembling heart
Crawls like the whisper of breaking into bud
Before the avalanche of wondering

Sometimes you are cold and beautiful
Like Narcissus
In the extravagance of your baroque eyelashes

Like a lump
The flaming cold
Ascends

Sometime sweet
In the midst of scents
Youth's secret hopes
From inferno to paradise
The noiseless path
Of warmth

NAIVETY

Before the stage when my thought stiffened in emptiness,
I had naively believed
That only politicians of George W.'s stripe
Instigated wails
Above the tired city,
Hypocrites and manipulators in chamber-pots,
The Andean vultures of a lower rank.
To defend the thesis
I paraphrased Zweig in the political encyclopedia.
In my poetry I built the stale philosophy
Of art before interest
And of ethics in the shaken dignity of true believers,
And of unity in the chaotic optimism of suffocation.

From Chomsky I asked the perfection of the feelings of perfidy
To determine the bond between the East and the West,
That political and disastrously efficient one.
And the boundary,
Like the Equator,
Which connects two distrustful halves.
Fists in the official salute
Of the economical West and the hungry East.

In Coquitlam the painter Bahic planted flowers
Next to the sculptures of Bill Reid.

Japan cannot possibly be the land of the rising sun,

Because the sun does not rise in the west.
It is shameful to suppress people
Within the boundaries of historical anachronism.

In the wheel of evolution
The fogs above the bewildered waters ...
The wisdom of the world
Moves in the alignment of heavenly people.
Maps and new shapings!

I was hoping for the time of flexible definitions
And not for the stink of burnt forests in the Okanagan,
Even if embraces were to disappear in the abysses of pleasure,
And love to create institutions of illustrated ceremony
Above the foul stench of profit and interest.

GREEN APPLES

They hoped, when reaching a real orgasm,
To discover the music of pleasure,
Polyphony,
But they
Caught the feeling of incompleteness,
Pleasure mixed with guilt,
Resignation.

The destiny of immature rubber plants
In the magic of life-scents …

If I am another leaf in the creation of your process,
Even a tiny ring in your chain,
I am leaving!
I am refusing the role of a link between the cars
Of a train speeding into the abyss of tomorrow.
I do not seek comfort in a questionable euphoria.
In that holy water is the curse
That the happiness in our hands
Is an illusion.

Up the hill to reach pleasure,
Delighted,
After the top, an abyss
Till the next hill,
A curse …

Our instincts are the wind
That shakes green apples
In the illusive light of a hallway.

BRANCH

Extending yourself like a hip
Rounded and warm
You bend
Bend
Beech branch

Coiling up in the sky

You wrapped your hair in the foggy dew
Helical branch
To be the one
The only one
In the shape of searching

Your skin is glistening and wet

How you did coil yourself
Like a viper
Beautiful
With fear in the eyes
With wind in the hair

THE BUILDER OF BRIDGES

Man is not a tree to stay where it is planted.
Even if he wanted to, he never does,
Or others do not let him.
If only he were a bird to return in spring
When a calamity is over.

I say, "Maria, not even birds return anymore whence they came.
It is the time of global warming
And nature's compasses are falling apart.
Not even elephants return anymore to die
At the places of their birth."

She looks somewhere through my eyes and whispers:
"There, for me, colors are colors, smells are smells
and bridges between two shores are bridges.
The bridge in Mostar won a victory over its destructors.
They ruined a five-hundred-year-old bridge,
And it resurrected young.
What builders build during the day,
A black fairy destroys during the night,
But the builders build it again the next day.
Even global warming cannot harm the bridge in Mostar,
So cannons can't either.
I used to work for Sarajevo Television and created programs,
Bridges between villages of our past. I do not know
If they were also destroyed by the gangs who first blew bridges
That bring people together.

They are blind to my bridges. I do not want to believe
They destroyed them. They did not succeed.
Bridges are hidden in the builders' hearts. And in their genes.
Evil men cannot pluck out people's hearts."

I speak again,
"Maria, you smuggled your bridges across the entire world
And seeded them here on the Pacific.
That is why Vancouver has hundreds of bridges.
These verses are the gifts to you from my heart."

The sea and the sky
Folded their arms over the harbour
And it turned into a pearlshell.
An old bridge shed a tear.
A purple distant light
Shone like a stone.

The verses say if the sea and the sky,
When smiling, can build pearlshells,
So can we. Again. Does it matter where?
Whenever you build a bridge between two shores,
It will touch somebody's heart.
And also the tear in the verse –
It springs from the builders' hearts.
To destroyers – cannonballs.
To builders – tears.
Till the end of time.

THE STORM

(Could a turbulent past start a prosperous future,
as a stormy night often precedes a rebirth of the sun?)

The other night furious howling of the wind
Tore away fledglings from their nest
And the whole night two birds with their eyes frozen
Fluttered through the storm
Devastated.

Darkness quivered under the glowing sky.

Last night an angry wind
Threw the nest into the stream,
Swollen with drunken waters,
Uprooting budding trees
Helpless
Along the frightened water's banks.

Gentle sounds of sleeping eyes
Disappeared in gusts of misfortune,
And curious shadows of light,
Nested in the branches,
Took refuge in dark cages.

The sun found the birds above the turbid abyss.

This morning fresh smells from cafés
Ran down the streets
With thrilling smiles in their bosoms.

RAINBOW

the bountiful harvest
in a charmed arch
of colors

the oasis of imagination
in the ceaseless impatience
of yearning

crimson
blue
light yellow
a surreal child of some miraculous union

in the heart
a primordial desire
of genetic wandering

MIXED TIMES

... And the old Herod became frightened of the prophecy:
In Bethlehem, the one who would take his kingdom had been born!
And legendary Herod ordered all young boys in Bethlehem to be
killed
And the prophecy to be forgotten.
He ordered !

A thought rings in my eyes,
A stare awakens in my nerves.
I turn into a tiny chip,
Frightened,
And sink in pain,
That has lived in my memory
Longer than pain.

On the streets,
Like a magic chime,
A bell quivers under the rush of sunrays.
In the mystical sound of brass the past awakens me.
I feel a hand above my head.

It chimes,
And the uneasiness in my hairs thickens.
My schizophrenic thoughts build entire worlds of the world.
As a storm breaks into the midst of sunbeams,
It rings in the light of my eyes,
And melts my images into a melody,

Into a colorful carpet of bells.

I mixed the times,
So I cannot recognize the one I live in.

SOLITARY MAN

In the heat of dreamy whispers
In the sway of dreaming grass
The grasshoppers feast

The headless azure sleeps

Downfield
Into the warm tremor dives an army of ants
The winds abate

The insolent stony grin
On the neck of the sleepy treetop
Of tomorrow's unending restlessness

Limousines light up the asphalt

Like some runaway child of the universe
Like the snowflake on the silvery canvas of frost
Across the field sails a solitary man

HEART IN ICE — CRYSTAL

Tell me, finally, on this drenched night,
In the whispering of wet streets,
In the fog of lost streetlamps;
Tell me, without the curse of morals, ethical dogmas,
Bullying you into an answer both civil and modest:
How long, how base, how crucifying,
Has your heart been telling you
That they tore you away,
You, wild, untrammeled flower,
You, proud as cornel-wood,
And threw you on a rock,
To thirst for the foaming water
Crashing against the rock,
So that this thirst makes you wither.

Tell me, without that cursed habit, shame,
Your desire to be caressed,
Say that none in this drenched solitude,
Unforgettable, carnal, enraged,
Broad yet confining,
Does not begrudge you,
Does not mercilessly descend upon your doomed freedom,
Upon your dignity, heritage, dormant roots
Beyond your reach.
Tell me, without feeling ashamed of yourself,
For your words are put under the symbols of others
(Nation, Religion, Murder),

Why do you sweat when dreaming?
Trembling! Distance!
You weak swimmer through politics and morals,
Politics and immorality! You swimmer!

Darkness in the depths, heights in the darkness!
Von Daniken and Asimov – foreign!
Heart in ice – crystal!
Does crystal have any use of itself?
Rhyme …

Say at least once,
While your brain is washed by slippery streets,
Roads of faith, the hopelessness of hope:
All humans are equal!
(God, the Party, Democracy!)

Thirsty shadows search for their faces
In the rainy night,
Tire tracks on the wet asphalt,
The butterfly in the hot lampshade,
Dry throat in the water …
Sirens proclaiming a race to the bitter end.
Pacifists on the Pacific, nations in Nietzsche,
Philosophy in madhouses, sinners on chariots,
You in me, with your eyes closed!

Steps full of time, passage in the impassable …

Tell me when they say your thought is uncivilized, apocalyptic,
That you are behind bars, silenced, disenfranchised,
Forced to the edge of the ocean, thirsty,
Imprisoned in a block of ice, sensitive,
Enslaved upon the Statue of Liberty,
On a wet road gazing at tire tracks, defrauded.

DROUGHT

Tree swinging against tree
The fir groves climb the pines
Covering them with their scent

The fields grin dryly
From rocky ground with blades of wig hair
Pleading for rain from the sky

Ray by ray made yellow
Among heads of over-ripe hemp
The milk-thistle grows alongside the sage bush

My bitter hopes
Left downstream to the abyss
Withered without a trace

DISOBEY THE LEADERS

(I wrote to the radio waves in the late spring of '92)

I address the people of Bosnian Krajina, my native soil.
I have the right to do this.
I have the right to address you,
More than those that recruit you
Under their war flags and banners.
Please, disobey those that intrude upon us their leadership
From now till we die –
Not a natural death, normal for every living creature
That leaves this world and finds courage to say farewells to his kin
As if entering a bouquet of flowers.
Stooping down to a tiny blue flower in the field
To whisper that he is leaving.

I address our people, all those whom my words reach,
For I do not corral people nor mark them with colors,
As they do with sheep.
I beg you, disobey the leaders
That drag us into death and destruction.
We hardly managed to rebuild what had been destroyed before,
And over our war cemeteries the grass has hardly grown.
It hasn't been long since the storks with long white necks
Trusted us again
And started building nests for their young on our roofs.

Europe proposes us as first among non-Western nations

To join their union and to renounce war.

When hearing their speeches at political conventions,
I ask how anybody can listen to them.
When seeing the direction they point their weapons at,
I ask how anybody can join their formations.
If we follow their banners
And turn the weapons at the direction they point,
Our mothers, sisters, daughters, and our native soil
Will wail again,
And the cemeteries and tombstones will grow anew.
Again, houses will burn,
And our cows and horses in barns.
Storks will once more leave our roofs.
There will be new poetry by a young generation of poets,
And new Nobel laureates will sing about our unhappiness.
How I wish they had never sung!
I do not like ashes and cemeteries.
I do not even like that Tito united the world at his funeral,
And that we, by his grave, were more glorious than ever before.

They are dragging us into the war against each other!
I swear, the blind lead us, the inferior and the revengeful.
They return to the past to take revenge,
They show the future and threaten,
Asking us to get even by paying with our blood.
They want church-bells and muezzins from minarets to hold our
wake.
I am afraid that those summoning us under their banners will,
As soon as the first bullet is fired,
Put the flag into the hands of others and hide in the shade.
And turn off the lights in our boroughs.
And fire from the darkness to draw us into mutual killing.
And we will kill each other, burn, and depart to foreign lands.

Those foreigners will rub their hands
And fill their pockets with our misfortune,

And send us parcels with the crumbs from their dinner tables
To gain the respect of their people and to repent to God.

We can change directions, adapt systems,
But not go to war!
War is nobody's brother, sister, or mother ...
War is the ugliest word among the ugly.
Disobey the parvenus that want to lead you,
And do not dirty your hands with the blood of other people.
Do not destroy what others have earned.
Do not build a world in which our children
Will visit us by our mass graves or tombstones.
Do not do unto others what you would not have others do unto you.
And do not offend God by laying violent hands on man.

The sound of the radio waves had barely faded
When bullets spilled blood on our sidewalks.

As a reward, the leaders spilled cooked corn over my head,
The corn cooked for Easter time,
And in front of my eyes started embracing people,
Accompanied by the wild tune
Of the old war marches and the new.

BLOODY ROSES '92

This summer our fields will go unharvested,
And the rosehips unpicked.
The sun set in early spring
And has yet to return
Upon our withered faces.

Yet we hoped for rain.

This summer, instead of horses
With scattered manes and extended tails,
Across our fields galloped tanks
And settled in our towns, their jaws open.

Our neighbors wore uniforms,
And raised their heads to the sky.

This summer, hearts stopped beating,
Eyes of the children running across fresh scented mountains
Died away.
Welcoming outstretched hands turned to shrieks.

On our paved streets
Bloody roses began to grow overnight.

This summer, our town's houses were torched
And whole neighborhoods went mute with bewilderment.

GEISHA

The tired sky opens to me.

On the crimson drapery of space
Flashes of lightning
Compete.
Smells wander
Through the paths of light.

A geisha
At the verge of tearful chastity
Lost in her thoughts.

People should blush
Because they stole the lights of stars
From humans.

If they gave me the kingdom of roses,
And the taste of honey on the tips of silicon breasts,
And power over the feelings in Vancouver's harbour,
I would sing on the empty deck of a ship
Lost in the arrogant harmony.

AHMED

They told me:
Ahmed,
Hit your head on the wall!
And I did.

They told me:
Ahmed,
Gather your bones!
And I did.

They told me:
Ahmed,
Jump with your bones into the fire!
And I did.

And then they said nothing.

PATRIOTISM

Was patriotism possible
In the last war in Bosnia?
And can patriotism sometimes be, even in
Deception, a feeling that brings people
To killing their compatriots?

Perhaps patriotism is a deception,
An ugly illusion
That drags masses into a slaughterhouse.
Perhaps it is like The New York Stock Exchange,
When they call some powerful big country a homeland,
And then a small one when they make it smaller,
And then a tiny one when they split it more,
And then some shit of a country
They call a homeland ...

Our children have gotten wings,
And Blanca already can fly on her own.
So it is easier when from the depths,
Somewhere from the homeland,
Familiar rock threatens out of darkness.

IN CASE OF CONTINUITY

At the onset of the first millennium
The native soil was
A cave of the crucified Christ.

At the onset of that other one,
When the shiny supernova fell apart,
The native soil rose above the pier.

The third millennium was waking up
In the distance of Galileo's telescope,
And a dark cloud on the sky above New York
Landed on the native soil
With a chaos from nothingness.

Today people are also odd,
Some new future is being born.
In the test tubes with the seeds of conception
Cloners do god's magic.
Civilization again sinks
Into a wistful music of Noah's ark.

BOSNIANS

I must have walked these woods a hundred times
Before I found you, my son,
Father's loop-eared sparrow!
Don't you remember how your ears were like wings
Before you became a man?

How hard this soil!
And ... different ...
I'm tired, son!
Uphill, downhill – a hundred times ...

And I thought you were with those below,
You know, over by that creek ...
I crossed the entire valley,
I recognized them all,
But ... no sign of you ...
I know that you were together,
Always ...

So ... why here?
Overhead the rotting beech trees
As if made of clay by children.
At your feet the eternal rock.
Its roots go deep.

Do you remember saying how the beech trees
Were like scarecrows in the night,

And how the green moss on the rocks
Reminded you of foreign lands?

Sweet thing, how could they?

I could not find your hand ...
Perhaps those below have it?
And why, misfortune, the right one?
The one that pulled my nose
And pinched my cheeks ...
And the eye!
Your piercing dark eye!
It too is gone ...
As if it had wandered off somewhere
Following the golden locks of some young girl.
Remember how your mother kissed your eyes
And how your sister teased you
For always milling about?

I searched for the two of them as well along the road,
But, nothing ...
Some newcomers mentioned
That they had left for America ...
You hear?!
Oh, my God! All the way to America!

And I ...
I am here, stroking your head ...
So unkempt, son, so unlike you!
I spent time in the camp,
On Manjaca ...

Some people moved into our house
And repainted everything.
Threw our houseleek from the roof!
You remember? The red one,
Whose oil we used to drop in your ear.

I don't think our dogs are still alive ...
They would have noticed me ...

Oh, dear mother! Oh, my God!
What's happened to us?
Who have we offended to deserve this?
Forgive me for weeping like an old woman.
You know I always frowned on that ...

I was thinking ... that when I found you
Together we would follow them
To America ...
And build ourselves an identical house ...
Makes no difference – Bosnia, or America!
But, I won't! ...
Who knows if we'd find them ...
America isn't over some creek,
Or the size of some village ...
I will build it here,
Under this beech tree!
For the both of us ...
So when they return ...
Oh, my son ...
We cannot even speak as before ...
I feel like I'm choking, suffocating ...
Something has me by the throat,
I don't know what, my son,
Father's loop-eared little sparrow! ... .

IF ONLY ...

How easily could I forgive you
That blood, the fires, the banishments,
If you had arrived from somewhere else,
Looked somehow different,
Had a different sensibility.

More easily could I forgive you
The grief you have caused us,
If you had crossed the seas,
From some other world,
In strange clothing,
Speaking foreign words ...

Perhaps I could understand
If we stood in the way
Of some unstoppable raving force
That grinds everything in its path,
Having come from the Urals,
Or the cold Russian steppes.

Less would I curse you
When I feel the scent of home
If you had come from the past,
With turbans on your heads,
Riding atop Anatolian horses ...

How horrified would I be
If you were of noble birth
And sullied your historical honor
With our blood!
Even if you were SS troops,
Or Black Shirts,
More easily could I forgive you
For the sake of future generations!

But you did not have to arrive on your satanic march.
You were here all the time,
Drinking from the same fountains,
From under the festive roses
Making toasts to friendship and brotherhood!

If only you had come from somewhere,
From afar,
Having sailed across seven seas! ...

DO YOU HEAR, OLD MAN?!

From the bed and into the dark of the cold night,
Encircled by fear,
Helpless,
A woman's whisper awakes:
Do you hear, old man? Someone's pup is howling …
All around, only frozen darkness
And the pup like a painful thought …

The woman turns, pushing him, yet he is motionless, no warmth.
A terrible thought turns in her head,
But she refuses, fleeing the thought.

See how quiet he's become …
As if hiding in the field of tall corn,
Quietly peeking through the hairy cornsilk
Toward the field of uncut grass
Where the two-legged raven-haired filly stood
Winking and taunting him …

She pokes him in the ribs, her fingers full of hope.

… That filly, old man …
Do you hear?
The pup's voice has grown feeble,
As if he's hungry,
Howling from hunger …

She nestles her body along his,
Only to be met by a cold numbness,
Like a big, a long icicle on their shingle house.

Why so stiff? You harnessed your pulses
As if caught in a tryst under the old apple tree.
So, your veins gone rigid, and your pulses turned silent ...
And all your fear, numb like your bones, old man ...
So, do you hear? Listen!
The pup's muzzle has gone rigid from the cold.
More of a wheeze now than a howl ...
Fear has gone to its mouth, and cold and hunger,
And these shells,
Falling all night upon the town.

I too was woken by a shell
And from my chest a hot stream gushed forth
But your sweet sleep would not let you wake ...

She leans her head upon his chest,
Only to be met by a mute chasm ...

And your heart has grown faint, my old man!
As if dreaming of our Jasmine,
As she is crawling out of that shell crater,
Where we buried her under blankets
To hide her from the cold and the starving dogs.

She screams and digs her fingers into his ribs.

Wake up! Don't frighten me!
That was no pup!
That was no bitch having pups in her death!
That was our Jasmine!
That was her trying to crawl out of the shell crater
Whimpering as if she came from the womb of a dying bitch
Hiding her from death in that there crater ...

She restlessly reaches around the stiff body,
Her fingers tear at the moist shirt.

Oh, dear God! Oh, old man!
This is not from my ...

This is from *your* chest!
The shell has opened this creek on your chest,
And it has overflown on to me ...

She rolls up to the dead corpse, whispering:

Wake me from this dream, dear God!
You cannot take him away from me too ...
Like some basket of cherries ...
Wake up, old man!
You cannot leave our Jasmine in that crater!

From behind the frosted window,
Someone's howling calls out again,
As if the bitch were having pups in her death.

SARAJEVO

In you, two worlds met,
Intertwined,
Like two white pearls in a purple shell:
Rosy-faced,
The trembling of the bodies from the sun's birthplace,
And golden sheaves of obstinate spirits
From the place where rum-colored light descends.

... And all the riches of the Eternal Trinity,
which noisily sail by on the haloes of the past.
Sleepy fountains by the skirts of the minarets,
Chiming sounds of the church bells,
And some strange tremor, Bosnian,
Obstinate and noble!

Virtuosos and craftsmen
Spent centuries building you,
Love songs in stone,
Outdoing one another in beauty,
Naming you after the royal palace.

You took in from all sides,
From all corners of the world,
The curious, the adventurous,
Offering a part of yourself,
Giving life to memories ...

V

At your peak
In the ecstasy of scattered centuries
Under the planet's fireworks,
The nations of the world gathered on your bosom
To take part in the modern dance of the Aegean south.

Under the linden's intoxicating scent
I dreamt of some lunatics,
Whom you sheltered in your bosom:
They rummage through your soul
And burn your hands;
The lightning bolt of human greed,
From the blind pupils of hate,
Destroys your centuries-old creations.

Somewhere from the wilderness,
From some dark corner of the mind,
They stoke fires upon your face.
Vultures circle overhead!
These rabid eagles of death spread their frozen wings,
And the sun goes dark,
And the river dries up,
And some strange tremor spreads out from your streets.

At noon, they hide the sun behind your majestic mountains,
They banish the moonlight across the Seven Seas,
Their clouds bring with them great sorrow,
Unbearable pain ...

Striking with hate upon you
To cripple your beauty,
To return your jewels to the dark depths.

Fiery tongues rummage
Through the intestines of antique structures,
Bascharshya burns!
Some inhuman scourge has risen from the Dark Ages
To wage its Satanic battle!

But you, metropolis, are stronger than hate
And, despite all of your suffering,
In your eyes I already see
Twinkling tears of hope.

A MARATHON BACKWARDS

New days of splendid perversions approach.
In kegs of frosted glass bitter liquid foams.
Grinning from shop windows,
People announce the continuity of defiant omens.

On lustful boulevards of sonorous extremities
Rave the smells of slit-carnation forests.
In the drawers of stolen flowers
Anguish. And colors
Driven out of the rainbow's spectrum.
Flags flutter over the faces of the statues of liberty:
Democracy with the aureole of genuine brazenness.

In the startled eyes of city facades,
In painters' canvases
Fatigue.
Under attack by world media – abysses:
Bosnia with tearful eyes, New York's new cemeteries,
Iraq in the eyes of the blind ...
A crimson feeling of closeness in chilled sensibilities.
A cosmic paradigm in people's encounters on sidewalks.

Broken processions march in the agony of their torrid directions.
Human bodies in the tufts of the new morality.
They drug philosophy in the palaces of fishy profit takers,
Priests rape boys in the seminaries of the Holy See,
They force women into the shells of butterfly larvae.

In the factories of Bill Gates' birthplaces of new intelligence
The future on its knees demonstrates a marathon backwards.

Whence a butterfly,
Delicate and timid,
Alights on the edge of a sonorous fountain
And whispers a song to the primordial elixir.
Love is bashfully being born on the benches in the city park.

EYES TO THE SKY

The hen-pigeon cradled all three of her chicks
In the shade,
Quenched their thirst with the water
From the cave's spring.

Next to the fire, the pigeons built their nests.

Three nights after midnight they wandered,
From the mouth to the source ...
A hundred hands holding one loaf of bread,
Clouds full of winter ...

All eyes look to the sky.
The stars wane.
On each forehead, as on a granite block of ice,
The universe engraved.

If the tear lived in a flower,
It would turn into an apple of ice,
At dawn the sun would set.

PATRIA

In the casino
Dark-skinned
Passionate
With the smile of the early flower
A stripper ...

It was a moist dawn above the oak tree

They moved out like bullets
Like seeds
Carried down-wind by desire
Moving fists full of partings

In dreams the scent of the grass on St. George's Day
Women's chirps turned into a flower
In the moonlight by the spring's magic spell
To some – a barge by the water
To some – the shadows of the moonlight
To some – gentle misty eyes
Trembling
All is melting
The field is budding
The seeds are sprouting

They scattered over the harbors
Down the metros
And left messages on train terminals

In spring feverish flocks of birds
Bring the smell of home

Our sights cross-eyed

The woman's dance slowly abates
As rain slowly stops
Or in the orchard's midst
The awakened night finds its strength

FEAR

The fire intertwined itself in their dawn,
Stripping the sleeping bird of its feathers ...
Forcing thorns into their eyes.

The moonlight dissolved the darkness.

Tree trunks everywhere like prison guards,
Yet the wild strawberry sprouts in the grove,
Spreading its warmth skyward,
As if regenerating the world with its heat.

This is not a maple forest.
The winds here have coughed much,
Scattering across the highlands
Green snow instead of evergreens.

Heads slowly boiling with silence.

Along the forest the fire creeps,
Freeing the horses of their heavy shoes,
So everything fertile in the rock will bear fruit.

NATURE'S CRY

The beech trees here have grazed away at the fields,
Multiplying downward
Across the highlands.

Here, both the heart and the sun are like the beech tree.

If one could have seen how the forest ignited in shame
When she was carried away,
How the hairy beech trees opened their umbrellas ...

If one could have sifted through the multitude
Of our neighbors
Who kill, through our split genealogy ...
If one could have snuck up on them
Without trembling eyes ...

The wolves mourned someone last night.

The beech trees have extended above the foul waters,
And their shadows,
Like time,
Sail away.

SLUMBERING LANDSCAPE

In the whispering of dry leaves,
Like an evil omen,
With eyes in the flight of birds,
Stone devouring youth.

Down the raving streams,
Like a pebble in the foaming crimson,
Deep tranquil thoughts.

A root at the twilight of arrival,
A gaudily baroque tree
In a season of drought.

Clusters of buttery dandelions,
Rising to the sun,
To a broken skull's astonishment.

FAILING TO DESCRIBE PAIN

I have never had the artistic gift to describe pain:
That indescribable state of human spirit
When the boy Meskan saw a blood stained knife,
A terribly sharp blade,
Coming closer to him in the hand of another man
Of the same human species.
Such great pain is beyond the power of my senses.
I am ashamed of my failing to describe the pain.
The pain when the boy,
Who was still running after butterflies,
Became afraid of pain.
The boy from Iris's story.
It does not matter. Any boy, or any human,
Or any living being on our planet.
Forgive me, you other beings,
For forgetting for a moment your pain.

The boy became afraid of pain when he lost hope.

They asked him for his name. And he told them.
And his ethnicity. And where he was from.
He told them everything he knew.
Something whispered to him that he was not guilty of anything.
And he had hope;
The way lightning is not guilty of its creation in the clouds.
Or hail, when in its helplessness it
Breaks young branches in orchards.

He was not guilty of his birth. Nor of the name given to him.
Nor of language and religion to belong to his people
As they belong to him.

I know his family.
They vowed neither to Jupiter
For placing anger before reason
And lust in the hearts of humans,
Nor to that half-witted Theutus,
A fierce enemy of the human race.
He knew he was not guilty
And he looked his headsman straight in the eyes.

The other had blind eyes. Vileness blinded them.
He was plowing his way to the future and happiness
With a knife. With a blade for Meskan.
To sacrifice him to the gods of war.
For good luck.
But God ordered Abraham, or Ibrahim,
To sacrifice a ram instead of a human.
God ordered!

That human being brought the knife's blade to Meskan's eyes
That he see its sharpness.
And the victim became afraid of pain.
Meskan turned his eyes away from the blade
And prayed to God to show himself,
And saw the Furies that throw snakes on people
And bring warmongering into human hearts.

The image of becoming afraid I can describe.
But not a boy's pain. Not such great pain.
I know of no words for pain so great as his.

Second Part

LIFE ON EARTH IS MERCILESS
IF I LOOK
AT IT THROUGH THE WINDOW
OF KINDNESS

I BECAME MORE INVOLVED WITH the Dalai Lama through my former neighbor and life-long friend, Osman Kulenovic. Formerly from Bosanski Petrovac, in Bosnia, and presently from Montreal, Canada, Osman told me how he had philosophically rounded up his life when meeting with the Dalai Lama in a Canadian province enveloped in separatism. I know that the difference between the Dalai Lama's Tibetan separatism and Quebec's is big, though if I were the leader of Quebec, or Tibet, I would rather seek to establish a fairly organized society than opt for separatism. It seems to me that a pluralistic society created with fairness in its structure offers more possibilities both for an individual and for the whole than does an atomized society. However, it is hard for me to get involved in politics since, like Daltonists, who are color blind, I am blind to national, religious and race differences, and seeking a politics without the residues of these -isms would be asking too much. If memory does not fail me,

because it was long time ago, Osman told me that he had asked the
Dalai Lama why he was trying to attain sovereignty for his Tibet in
a peaceful way. The Dalai Lama had replied that each of us is first
a human being and then a member of a nation, and that the biggest
human sin is to take up arms against other people. I tried to persuade
my fellow Bosnians of this in their bloody mutual conflict near the
end of the twentieth century, and the only result of my attempt was
my intimate extension of that belief in non-violence to get closer to
the Dalai Lama's philosophy.

A long time later, I was granted a meeting with one of the legends
of civilization at the turn into the third millennium, not somewhere
on the gorges of the Himalayas but on the mountain Gabel Musa, the
Mount Sinai of tradition, from where a keen eye can see the shores
of the Mediterranean around Gaza and the domes of the holy build-
ings in Jerusalem. That arid mountain giant was more for a Buddhist
monk than for me, if we were ranked according to our aptitudes for
asceticism. Also, for those 4,000 steps to the top one needs a younger
heart and younger legs. I have always wondered how the old Moses,
or Musa, found strength to climb to the top of that mountain. I once
believed that God, in the form of a burning bush, helped him so that
He could reveal to him the Ten Commandments and the laws of Israel.
If one is to believe in that tradition, God did not choose that place by
chance, and if my logic is correct, He cannot forget that place, so
He even now from the top of Gabel Musa watches how people of
that part of the world are killing each other. I, however, believe that
He is not happy because people do not follow the commandments
revealed to Moses. When they told me that I had to go to the top of
holy Sinai's mountain in order to meet somebody very important, it
dawned on me that the instruction had something to do with God's
presence on top of those deserted, barren mountains.

First, an already dried-up Mediterranean wind brought to me the
words that arrested my final climb to the top of the craggy mountain
boulder covered in crimson dust:

"There on those ascetic hills, and in those fertile oases down there,
for centuries people have been competing to see who will get closer
to God. Or, who will conjure a more daring image of God and his
apostles, who will write down more of God's commendations and

regulations in order to rule over people more successfully." His soft face, his eyes gracious with serenity and respect, appeared beyond the words. He was sitting on a stone, surrounded by the crimson rocks and was looking at me.

No doubt it was he, the Dalai Lama, a man not a god, as he himself has been saying in his defense against being made equal to God. I had not expected that here I would meet the most famous Buddhist monk in history, who stormed through the world of philosophy, religion, and goodness in the turbulence of the third millennium's dawn. He was wearing a splendid long cloak made of a shiny dark brown fabric and on his left hand was wearing beads of the same color. He had that something that made his face recognizable even in the mist on top of Gabel Musa – a mild discoloration around his eyes. There was no doubt it was he, despite the cloud trying to conceal his always-optimistic face.

Or who can think of a more genuine and powerful deity in the struggle for survival? I felt that my face was turning red because I understood that I had said something that might have sounded like blasphemy, and that I might have offended his holiness. To say the least, I might have acted crudely by turning the conversation toward things that have always interested me.

"People have the ability to create." Saying this, the Dalai Lama accepted the conversation, indicating to me to sit on a flat stone, like a step in front of him.

dalai lama: Not only in their material world but in the spiritual world of imagination as well. In history, preceding the times of turmoil were the times of fear for survival. Those are the waves in the human consciousness after which come changes, as when a metal is heated until it melts, so it is poured into new forms that for a long time serve those who did the melting. Fear and struggle for survival have strongly motivated people to bond with deities. In moments of the most fierce struggle for survival leaders have reached for God's help in order to unify and motivate people. Then people spread that idea among themselves, or imposed it, or stole it from each other, or simply let the air blow it away and used it as weapon or hope. How did that thought come to my mind? To me wind is a servant of time, its herald. It reminds me of the stream of our thoughts through time, of that which is unattainable and so liberated that there is no way it can be enslaved and prevented from performing its function. If they were to put a wall in front of it, it would spread its breath beyond the wall, like that flow of air creeping from Gaza and Jerusalem, from the oases of the modern civilization inundated with hatred. It is unnatural that hatred dominates in oases since they are natural sanctuaries of hope and life. I do not blame those who, in the struggle of life, make or invent some kind of protection for themselves and for their kin, related to them either by love, birth, or simply by desire to live in society – which is easier than to live alone.

He was talking and looking into the depths as if seeing through the centuries long gone.

It seems to me it would be easier if we did not have such an ability to create. I let it out spontaneously. Human creativity led people to usurp the role of nature. People nowadays create artificial brains. We are the contemporaries of the Kingdom of Bill Gates, and whole generations of cloned, synthetic beings are to come. I fear to call them human beings. What will the invasion of these creatures do to the human gene pool? What will happen with them during a collapse of technologies, a simple electricity black out? What path will the religions born in these mountains take? What is going to lead people and stimulate them to create laws which do not alienate them from nature?

"Ha, ha, ha …" laughed the Dalai Lama and offered me something that looked like the withered root of some plant.

dalai lama: Chew this. This plant slows down the thinking and prevents thoughtlessness. We, there in the mountains, believe that it successfully prevents blood from clotting and brain strokes. You ask questions that your offended Creator would ask. I, somewhere in the cradle of my faith, hold onto the last defense. Maybe there is a mechanism that won't allow the transformation of humans into some other kind of beings. I believe that in the genes governing the paths of development there are regulations and limitations. I think that spontaneity is not infinite. I also feel that a rapid technological explosion is a burden for civilization. People have become obsessed with material values, which is not good because it provokes abuses of all written and unwritten laws and brings other evils. Material possessions are sweet only for a short time. Spiritual ones are long lasting. Craving material possessions works against basic elements of harmony. In our time we can find a lot more harmony in primitive societies than in cities and in economically developed societies. Traditionally organized societies have more harmonized interactions. Urban societies are disharmonious. Material development of the world is not an advantage in the new millennium because it causes the disappearance of harmony and a comfortable, quiet way of life.

For a moment his face looked to me like that of a being beyond temporality, like some strange mummy hidden somewhere in the trembling heights above the Earth rather than in the depth of Earth's sand and rocks.

dalai lama: Caravans were passing along the roads down there long before concrete paving. They say Moses came out here when he left the Nile delta behind. Caravans went from the East to the West, from the West to the East. People used the roads more attentively than they do in our time, when cars speed as fast as the eye's glance.

The Dalai Lama was talking and looking into the depths as if trying to make out an old caravan.

Because of hatred. Thoughtlessly, I continued to provoke Tenzin Gyatso, the 14th Dalai Lama. *Here where the philosophies of the encounters with God began, from where they disseminated and conquered the world, here people hate each other terribly. How is that possible? How can God allow so much hatred among people, especially here where they erected the greatest sanctuaries for him?!*

dalai lama: I have a different view on what you are calling God. If by that you mean a creator, or a stimulation for doing good deeds, than that must be inside a man. The man has to discover and cherish that in himself. If some selfish interest prevents him from doing that, then he is living a deception. A lie. And if that is the case, then it does not matter where the two of us are sitting: above Jerusalem, in Bosnia, or in the Antarctic. I mentioned Bosnia, where your roots are. I know the dean of the Franciscan Theological University in Sarajevo, Mile Babic. Mile Babic said that he did not care whether a politician is an atheist or believer. For him it is important that a politician is a good and honest man since, as he said, it cannot be rationally proven whether God exists or not. Faith is a personal matter for an individual. The worst thing is to link a faith with a nation or with a political interest since narrow nationalistic politics spread fear, one person feeling threatened by another. Spreading fear of others generates irrationality; people behave like sheep running into their corral. I think it is positive that both atheists and believers follow Babic's thoughts. The problem is not because people are of different races, nationalities, religions and cultures. The problem is that people economically exploit and politically subjugate each other. The differences among them are the treasures of civilization, and vile deeds against each other are the evils.

An eagle above our heads started to call so energetically that I thought it wanted to draw our attention to something that we needed to see. We looked at the sky and followed its circling; we saw its eyes forever focused on the earth.

"They do not change as fast as people," commented the Dalai Lama without diverting his gaze. "Human technology does not force their spiritual change."

To me they are similar to people in some way, I said. *They instigate fear and they kill.*

dalai lama: In the eagle's case, how can I say it, the Creator is to blame. He made them unable to survive without devouring other creatures. Eagles normally do not eat other eagles. In our case, we humans are the guilty ones. We could survive without killing, but we do kill each other. And once that process begins, it cannot be easily changed. When we make a mistake, we cannot turn the clock backwards and start from the beginning.

Many of those oases down there are not developed. They are ruled by tradition, but hatred prevails there. In those barren places people hate each other, but praying to God and following the laws of their religion is sacred to them. In their holy scriptures, hatred, killings and summons to killing abound. Maybe because of that you talk about Buddhism more as a philosophy than as a religion.

dalai lama: Oh, no! Maybe I have not been precise enough. The creators of religions are human. And Buddhism has been created by people. Religions and philosophies are like their creators.

Is Buddhism really something else?

dalai lama: It is different in many aspects. Don't get me wrong. We do not want any domination, neither over material possessions nor over the human spirit. Our philosophy is not a conqueror's. We crave spiritual peace and happiness, but if one conquer and imposes, in such an act there is pain and hatred. Man's highest moral obligation is to snuff hatred in himself and to resist the ambition to dominate other people. Human society should not be based on profit and domination.

We live in a world of modern societies, far from primitive human communities. Behind us are millennia of human civilization. However, we have always had the same problem: as soon as one human society achieves a high power, it attacks others and destroys them. Could it be possible for one society to change that rule? To achieve great power but to not misuse it? To not impose itself by force? I tried to provoke more practical answers.

dalai lama: The formation of military powers in our time stems from the beginnings of human social organization. People form and use military power because of the absence of spiritual revolution.

Maybe the reason for this is that it is easier to improve technology than the human spirit! Not even in this day and age do people have a branch of psychology that explicitly studies the disciplining of the human mind to be good to other people. People have always been taking from and killing each other. All big invasions in human history have started in the same way. If we consider our civilization only from Graeco-Roman times, when the first institutional attempts at humanism and democracy appeared, there are too many examples of evil. The Roman Empire expanded into a mighty power and spilled its might over neighboring people, not with the purpose of bringing happiness, but to subjugate, plunder and exploit in the most inhumane manner. The Mongolians became a huge military power, and their Khans went around the world like a destructive torrent. Then Alexander the Macedonian, then Arabs, then the Turks, then the Austro-Hungarians, then Hitler and then Nazis, then ...

Then Americans in recent time, at the dawn of the third millennium, according to the Western calendar, I jumped in instinctively and a little incoherently; *not even Americans, the dominant people of the modern era, can avoid the curse to grow into a mighty power and then to go around the world destroying and killing other people. Since my youth, I have believed that Americans would lead the world toward peace and happiness because they consist of all of us, all peoples of the world. But instead they use the most modern weapons against people everywhere. In today's world they do not have a rival, so it would be most natural for them to offer the world recipes for peace and happiness, not for war and hatred. In their fight against other people only they have used the most terrible weapon of mass destruction – the atomic bombs dropped at Hiroshima and Nagasaki. And those bombs were not directed at military targets but at civilians. They, like those before them, try to decorate their warmongering with the aura of a humanitarian mission and the attainment of happiness for other people, but they mercilessly kill around the world. Now, when civilization is entering the third millennium, the Americans, with their vaccines for happiness and peace for all, block United Nations' resolutions aimed at preventing the militarization of the universe so that they can place their weapons of mass destruction above the Earth. Is it, asks Noam Chomsky, because through the doctrine of hegemony over our planet, they want to ensure their survival? In his powerful nation Bush Junior has even succeeded in institutionalizing the perpetual right of the United States to militarily eliminate any challenge in the world directed against American global hegemony. Bush's modern pirates went to Iraq with a mighty military power to plunder its riches and to secure dominance in that part of the world for the sake of profit and energy resources. For this purpose they lied to their own people and to the rest of the world that they were against terrorism and against weapons of mass destruction. Very similar to Slobodan Milosevic in the former Yugoslavia.*

I realized that I had been ranting, but felt the Dalai Lama was satisfied. And he was so direct in replying:

dalai lama: I would like to embed in the human spirit automatisms for being good to other people, a mechanism to oppose bad leaders, regardless whether people chose them freely or were forced to accept them. The human mind can do that if each individual thinks about it and gives it precedence over petty selfish interests. People can choose the good and reject the evil if they want.

I had something to add. *In general, human society through history has abounded in revolutions. Its development has not been organic, but revolutionary. When a system swells and stretches its coating to the maximum, an explosion ensues that destroys interactions and creates the conditions for a new system on a different foundation.*

dalai lama: But those revolutions are only in the material world: economical, technological and social phenomena. The real revolution of human society results from the changes within the human spirit. If people could really understand that each man's task is to take care of the happiness of others, and if each individual would behave in such a manner, it would create a genuine feeling that each man is useful and welcome. Instead of hatred and fear for survival, human society should cherish a good heart in people. When each individual considers all human beings equal to him/her, and recognizes their desire for happiness and their right to it, he/she will automatically feel sympathy for and closeness to others. We have to learn to work not only for ourselves and our families or nations but also for the well-being of all others. Universal responsibility is the best foundation for the happiness of each individual and for peace in human society.

I tried to follow the Dalai Lama's thoughts. *Does that mean the lack of spiritual revolutions leaves individuals at the mercy of material revolutions, that it constantly forces them into the struggle for survival in which all people are the same? The basic problem of civilization so far has been the insecurity of the individual. That state of human spirit leads man to losing faith in himself, so a person's mind starts craving for a leader and defender and reaching for God*

dalai lama: In the past religion and morality were closer. Nowadays many people believe that science defies religion and lessens the human need for God. I think that science illuminates the path for people, but it does not reduce human fear. If all religions were now to disappear, human society would find itself in chaos. If each human being had his/her own philosophy, if there were no generally accepted beliefs and moral norms, chaos would be inevitable.

Does it mean that religions are indispensable in human society and that without these systems of beliefs there would be no happiness and security?

dalai lama: Although I am a high priest of one religion, I think that it does not matter very much whether a person is religious or not. It is more important to be a good man. I am first a Tibetan and then the Dalai Lama, and I am first a human being and then a Tibetan. As the Dalai Lama, I have a special responsibility for Tibetans, and as a human being, I have a much bigger responsibility for the entire human family where we all belong.

If we all were thinking like that, there would not be hatred and killing in those sanctuaries down there. We could say that we were the progeny of God's creation. But, as it looks now, it seems that the

Bosnian Heretics were right when they said that Satan had created men.

dalai lama: People are people. It is not important what we think about who created people. What make us unique in the living world on Earth is our mind and feelings. We do not have to accept religion as a source of morality, but there must be some means that would teach people the difference between the good and the bad, the honest and the immoral, and that would show what stimulates a positive and what a negative attitude. For the human race, it is essential that we know that the aggression toward others is wrong exactly because every human being wants to be happy and to avoid suffering. We all desire a good life, but it does not only mean to have good food, clothes and protection. That is not enough. We need good motivations: compassion without dogmatism, without a complicated philosophy; a simple understanding that other people are our brothers and sisters, and a sincere respect for their rights and human dignity.

A high percentage of people belong to one of the religions. All great religions of our civilization emphasize that the foundation of human existence is peace. However, people, those religious people, have been raising arms against each other, now as in the past, and have been killing each other. I like Erasmus of Rotterdam's words about war: "War is such a cruel thing that it suits wild beasts better than people; such mindlessness that poets imagine it came from the Furies; such a plague that it leads to a general corruption of customs; such injustice that it could be waged only by the worst bandits; and such a godless affair that it has nothing in common with Christ and his teaching."

dalai lama: I know, and I am a leader of one of the world's great religions. People have been praying to God for thousands of years, and haven't come closer to peace even for one smallest unit of time; on the contrary, sometimes high religious priests take a lead in waging wars, regardless of how contrary that is to the basic laws of their religion. Because people are like that. There hasn't been a great spiritual progress in human society. We all need peace. But we need an honest peace based on mutual confidence and the realization of the truth that we, brothers and sisters, need to live together, without attempts to destroy each other. And also when a nation or a society is different from another one, there is no alternative but to live with one another. And it is much better to live together in happiness. People will always have different views and interests, but the only intelligent way to negotiate interests and different views is real dialogue. Promoting the culture of dialogue and non-violence for the future is the fundamental revolution in our civilization. World peace depends on the peace in people's hearts. War is like fire where people serve as fuel. One example is the conflict in the former Yugoslavia. We could see how a relatively minor quarrel quickly set the whole region on fire. That is because people have failed to learn that the nature of war is cold cruelty and suffering ... Yes! Very sad is the truth that religions have been the major source of conflict in human history. It is like that in our time too. Religious fanaticism and hatred leave behind killed people, destroyed communities, and destabilized societies. How to prevent that? It seems banal, but religious institutions need to retreat from political institutions and to occupy themselves with instilling spiritual values in people such as LOVE, COMPASSION, PATIENCE, TOLERANCE, FORGIVENESS, and HUMBLENESS. That will certainly help people to become good human beings.

The Dalai Lama had enclosed his thoughts in a circle of happiness, whispering not ten new commandments but comments on how people can enhance their spirit. I was not in the mood for comparing the whisper of the Buddhist monk with the commandments revealed to Moses. They were spoken in different times, at different stages of the development of human society, but are very similar. Why did the Dalai Lama speak like that at the dawn of the third millennium? For a couple of thousand years, between Moses and this 14th Dalai Lama, have people not learned to respect the Biblical God's commandments? Why is a Buddhist monk on the sacred mountain fighting for a spiritual revolution of human society? For the same goal our God's commandments have had? Instinctively I looked at the monk's face and discovered a trace of uneasiness in his gracious eyes. I supposed that he had had enough of the conversation with me and that

I somewhat tired and bothered him, and involuntarily I let a protest slip my tongue:

It is easy for you, having grown up on your heights, on those un-reachable heights of the Himalayas. From there you have been giv-ing advice to the rest of the world. You are like Moses, who climbed Mount Sinai and gave advice to the Israelis. And you have climbed the much greater heights of the Himalayas and have given advice to the whole world. It is easy for you because those in your south have given you a spiritual joy, and those in your north a strange patience from the past. It is easy because they entrusted you with the symbols of the good that adhere to the reincarnations of Chenrezig, heavy with gold and wisdom. It is easy for you, Dalai Lama, because you are not troubled by the question why the boats from the heights of the Andes, with the mystical descendents of the alien Oryana, have chosen to come to your Tibetan slopes of God's mountains. Because on your back you do not carry the Balkans' unhappy triangle, where the square on the hypotenuse is not equal to the sum of the squares on the two shorter sides, or simply: What if man has profaned the spirit woven into the gardens of his body?

I did not notice when a cloud above our heads descended between us. I had a thought that maybe it wasn't the Dalai Lama I had been talking to; that I had been in some state between a dream and rapture, and that somebody much more powerful then a human being had en-twined with my mind. Was it the ghost of Erasmus who had arranged my meeting with the Buddhist monk? Or was it somebody who did not care about our individual happiness or unhappiness that much but was interested in global questions about the human race; somebody who must have used a carriage beyond the reach of my eyes to land on that dry mountain top; somebody from some other world without the hatred among the beings on top of the life-ladder on Earth; or somebody who had come to check how Oryana's descendents behave on this planet? But the voice of the Dalai Lama rippled the cloud between us, and I heard his parting words:

dalai lama: Man was given a mind to use: a mind of special quality. Creative and inexhaustible. The mind should dominate over man's passions and prevent the mistreatment of others, especially when it brings evil onto other people. That is my true religion. In that sense, there is no need for a temple, a synagogue, a mosque or a church. There is no need for a complicated philosophy, a doctrine, or a dogma. Our very heart and our mind are the temple ... The doctrine is compassion, love for thy neighbors, and respect for their rights and dignity regardless of who and what they are. Yes! That is what we need. As long as we practise this doctrine in our daily lives, regardless of whether we are learned or not, whether we believe in Buddha or God or follow some other type of religion or no religion at all, as long as we feel compassion and responsibility for others, no doubt we will be happy. In that case we would not need the verses: *Do not say people deserve war / whence came such a grotesque idea?*

The last words of the monk sounded like the shriek of an eagle. Instinctively, I lifted my head towards the sky and saw him circling up high. Truly, he was shrieking as if to warn us of something. When I returned my gaze to the speaker, he was not there anymore. Even the cloudlet that had been between us had moved to the side where the path to Jerusalem and Gaza led. I was surprised at his disappearance. Even annoyed. I hadn't succeeded in finishing the conversation the way I had imagined at the moment I met the Dalai Lama. I wanted to provoke him to tell me if he was worried about humankind at the awakening of the third millennium. If he was worried that the biggest military power shamelessly marches in front of the Statue of Liberty because the leaders of America have turned it from the world's hope into the world's fear and into one of the world's most hated nations. I wanted to confront him more seriously with Chomsky and his warning of the danger of unbridled imperialism. I wanted to ask him if he was afraid of the superpower in the hands of a sick and greedy mind and of a profit-blinded democracy. What has happened to the human spirit? Is the hope in a spiritual revolution of civilization self-deception? And how is it possible to achieve a balance between reason and passion? According to ancient legends, Jupiter is to blame. He gave man twenty-three parts of passion and only one of reason. If such is the disproportion between the material and the spiritual, then is it realistic to expect a spiritual revolution to lead humans to lasting happiness? Thus, without the Dalai Lama, on top of sacred Mount Sinai, I am left with my poems only. Hatred, like a terrible disease of the human psyche, is more devastating for the human race and life on Earth than all natural cataclysms, even more than the fluorescent teaching of Stephen Hawking that the universe came about in the beginning of time and will disappear in its end.

I SING IN THE RAIN

I sing in the rain
And do not mind that it never ends,
Streets are soaked in water born from the sea.
To me this rain is still warm from yesterday's sun.
Through the tiny drops of rain I travel toward that sun.
Yes, I am happy!

My song climbs the arc of raindrops
Before they hit the watery streets.
In the fear-soaked moments
Up along the slant of their fall my clouded song
Finds in that stormy cloud
A glittering crack to the blueness of the sky
Bathed in sunshine.
Yes, I am happy!

I sing
And rain is dripping on my glasses
And the warmth of my eyes fogs the thick lenses.
Along my wet forehead wrinkles
Ridged with the past
Ripple,
But my gaze
Wins its battle with myopia
And through the foggy glass flows up
To the sun riding above the rain.
Yes, I am happy!

I sing that happiness is not a stifled candle,
Its life fading in the flame,
That gives light only so long as the flame burns.
Onto my happiness they wanted to shackle the past,
The stone biography of memory.
But happiness scaled the elevator shaft of their schemes
And poured down the paths of my gaze filling my eyes,

Like Phoenix born from cinders
Scattered over the sea.

To me the song is Cousteau's barque
And carries me through each new life it sings.

MOMENTS FOR LOVE

They'd awaken him with a fragrance of garden roses,
Bringing memories of childhood
Under the window of his granny Persa.
The agony in the hallway of General Hospital ...
Vancouver brushes up for the Olympics.
The Liberals compose the anthem!

Bato shuts both of his eyes.
Through the clenched teeth of his struggle for life
The verses of George Payerle rustle:
It is enough
Neither for the beginning nor for the end.

He isn't glad of the end.
The beginning was closer to his feeling for life.
He reminds me of a Gypsy song
In the smoke-filled inn of my sentimentality:
Let us not rush toward Balkan fields of red peony,
Toward the unknown beyond our grasp.
The beginnings are permeated with hope,
The endings with desperation.

His struggles were Odysseus's dilemma:
Nymphs or Penelope ...
Uncertainty behind the foamy wave,
Or the marble obelisk on Ithaca.
We both loved minute moments of time

And shared Hadrian's frustrations
And the feeling that at journeys' ends,
Even if covered with roses,
Beyond greatness and sensibility
Abysses await.

And in times of trouble small things are life-gifts,
In illness, the moments when pain sleeps.

I feel his shudder. And fear.
And again the feeling of passion. His reincarnation ...
He reacts to the buzzing of bees drunk with blossom.
Tell me your poems, he whispers.
I need new moments for love.
I cannot have enough,
Neither for the beginning nor for the end.

MUTATION

Nash introduced to mathematics
The obsession of imaginary life.
To the numbers thirty and fifty
He gave the loft of vernal winds
And into set theory gathered all learning.
In division, he pictured worlds.
When they diagnosed a schizophrenic intuition in him,
He was drawing the geometric progression of points.
Asked about the inverse of history,
He declared hope for the equality of instincts.

He dreamed of anthems
And bannered flags
In a futurist Freudian agony,
Churchbells at the museum gates of the revolution
On the red square of dreams.
Someone's new table of multiplication
Frightened him,
And color-matching in the rainbow's spectrum
Drove him into the zone of arithmetic mutation.

All along
The margins of his consciousness
Some children played the wheel dance
In Nash's collection of identities.

Mystic genius, throughout the night he laughed

At the unknown in the theorem of accumulation.
For him the calculations played by tipsy pianists
Are preludes to the theme
In the abyss of a mindless civilization.

GIFT

Last night in my dream full of dreams
I saw my imagination. I dreamed of my feelings.
And of selfish hope.
I saw Mount Osjecenica, from my youth, from Bosnia,
With its bare rocky head.
I saw it in the icy Canadian North.
In the mountains of the Yukon. Transplanted.
Closer to me.
As if it were bathing in the clear waters of Vancouver
Harbour. In my pride.
My yearning brought it from there.

I dreamed of giving it to Una and Adrian,
My descendents in the cold North.
To Una, the most beautiful girl in the world,
Even if judged by the eyes of others.
And to Adrian, too serious and bulbous,
Who has already pronounced the word "da-da"
Both in the language of his forefathers and in English.
I see, and nostalgia comes out through my sweating,
Our very Balkan faces climbing my mountain
And pulling a sled,
Like other children on the ice of North
Under the sky adorned with the lanterns of stars.

I have always wanted my descendents to pull sleds
Up Mount Osjecenica,

No matter where on our tiny planet.

I wonder why,
Against my will,
Tears run down my face
In my last night's dream.

THE SMELL OF DUST

When I close my eyes in early spring,
The smell of dust brought by the wind of my youth
Brings the feeling that time stands between me
And the images beyond the frame of transience.
It seems to me that time pushed me away
From those bright colors on paintings
Of merciless passing.
But not the feeling when I see again
How we flew kites
Mixing with dust in the wind,
The one that blows from the south.
We flew them down the field together
And we did not know
That we belonged to different tribes,
And even if we had known, it did not matter.
The smell of that old dust was hiding
The whole winter in my joy.

When I close my eyes in the dawn,
While the sun opens the eyelashes of its dreams,
I feel the smell of smoke coming out of the bosom
Of our worm-eaten shingle houses,
A long time ago when we would sit at the table,
Both together Muslims and Christians,
And first gnaw barley and corn bread
To later earn a heap of Ramadan and Christmas treats,
And when we swore only by Tito's name

And by our mountains,
That we'd always love each other.
In front of my closed eyes passes dust in the wind of time,
The dust that stays when the wind abates
In the imagination of my joy.

Behind my closed eyes awakens the feeling
That all the people in this world
Came from the same joyfulness,
From that elixir in our spirit
We all crave and hope for,
Like long-necked glasses
That are happy only if filled with wine,
And wine-drunk travel through our lives.

COLORS ON FACES

Daltonists walk the streets
Through the steaming spectrum of destructive colors.
For them black and white are equal
And reflections of imagination in their splendor.

Marvelous colors of the butterfly's wings
Waft insight to my intuition. Messages …
Pacifists pray on the streets.
Hands draw flowers on the pavements. The happy call out.
Smells instead of colors on our sleeves.
Mevlida Karadza in the carriage of bliss.
The end … And the beginning of the new century.
The song on the streets of Lille. On pavements,
The French draw the characters
From the Diary of the People of Sarajevo
At the end of the century of extremes.
Her one hand clutches at the roots of survival,
The other a new life by the Pacific.

The Eiffel Tower in clouds.
Magdalena at the mercy of the expelled.

The colors on people's faces are a challenge to me,
Something pagan in the nightmarish civilization.

At the Sorbonne, Mevlida demonstrates.
She did not choose the colors on her face,

Nor to be born in the midst of spring
In the old wooden house under the golden apple,
Nor to have a kerchief wrapped around her head,
To be blessed with sacred water.
Winds borrow the fragrant color of the curses
Electrifying the hairs of her defiance,
And push her outrage through the turbulent times,
Above the cascades of her feelings.
My colors are stolen from the reaped fields,
Torrid,
The last whispers of the sun over the roofs of our past,
Triumph in the snowy avalanches of destiny.
The springs of merry notes
In the melodies of the cheerful.
The faces are only
These and those,
Imaginative moves of ballerinas
In my wide open eyes.

SNOWFLAKE

the tiny flame
in the icy storm
of wondering

the confused jester
solitary
floating like a smile
in the gray shadow
above dew-imbued hopes

the glitter of the blossom in the eye
on the furrowed brow
in the hair
the easing of the raving of frozen scents

it strides down the cobweb of dusk
big headed
toward the unkind canvas of dawn

in flight
the flower of crystal anxiety
without stems
in a snowdrift
deceased bird of the universe

THE POET

The poet is not just a man
Even if he had the entire planet in his head
And all the riches of the Larousse Encyclopedia,
The programming of all possible genes,
Senses for various virtues ...
In his visions thrive the instincts of future creations,
In his imagination – prophecies.

The poet is a museum of different worlds.
It gathers the mighty, and the tiny ones.
The bygone.
Across his mind run rivers;
On his lips call silent winds
That bend the shoulders of bony mountains;
And joy, grief, tremor and yearnings,
Shameless dreams of the crafty fingers of ploughmen
And fruit-growers,
Circus jongleurs, tennis players,
Painters and con men,
Rich dimwits,
Profiteers ...

The poet's eyes are mirrors
Teeming with longing glances,
Sighs and tears,
Boundlessness.
In his ears echo the whispers of the pious

Awakening the symbols of their hopes,
And the crippled ones
When inaudibly praying for their extremities
To grow in their sleep ...
In the poet's senses teem the emotions of escape
When the beheaded life turns to horror,
And the encounters
When the sun's rays entwine with dark shades.
In the poet's realm
Instincts clash,
Identities scream,
As if thunder wondered over a severed flower.
There reign spectrums of artificial hues
In the tearful eyes of the sexually colorblind.

In the depth of his eyes
The harmony of the world,
In the breath of his heaving lungs
Chaos and curses.

The poet breathes life into words
And turns words into life,
Into an ever changing, keener feeling.
His creations
Are the essences of creations,
A sweet elixir from the sea of life.

The poet is Marko Vesovic,
Delighted with the pride of the wounded,
And George Bowering with the instinct to see things
In a constant motion.

SERENADE

I do not really want
All things to turn into desire.
I do not want all my delight
To come only from joy.

Since birds became strange
In a magic breath of wind,
Street encounters
And nature's spring call
Have become my wishful thinking.

In this world I plead for drops of glitter
From the clouds.
In despair when I awake
I seek refuge in a dream without despair.

I do not believe in colorful deceptions.

When I feel I am but a grain of sand in an hour-glass,
I force my imagination to stope
The fatal abyss
At the hour's waist.

In the past, all is past.
For the future I need hope.
But in every present moment,
As moments live their lives

I'm sure that I myself
Sing my own life's serenade.

WHEN OUR LIPS TOUCH

When our lips touch,
Our eyes darken,
And all the gates
Welded by our hands
Open.

When our lips touch,
Our chests tremble,
And the burning fire
Travels down fertile fields.

When our lips touch,
Reality is transformed into a dangerous flame
And grain ripens once more.

In lips' trembling touch
Rare seeds begin to sprout,
And, with their buds,
They enter
Our worlds.

RAINS IN THE ROSE GARDENS

It is March. This one too brought the weather
Of wind-stripped waves in the open sea.
Rain is rain even when it falls silently and monotonously.
This one sneaks from the dreary grayness of the sky
And night creeps into the moist darkness
As skillfully as profiteers creep into our pockets,
Like the nostalgic voice of Sarah McLachlan,
Spontaneous breath of my contacts with nature.

I know youth does not accept boundaries
And instincts rule the planet.

Blanca, too, changes spontaneously,
By the miraculous law
I used to notice only in others' children.
The heat in the eyes of my little girl frightened me
While she turned invitingly
For a group of grade-ten boys.
Neither their clothes nor their game
Reminded me of the time of my youth.
The difference between us scared me
And their freedom without filters,
And their rose-powdered cheeks.
They did not care if,
And where, and when,
Some crack-brained politicians might pull us into the fighting
Of masses against masses,

Or that this was the third year
Of Bush's rampage in Iraq.

I believed I knew youth does not accept boundaries
And instincts rule the planet.

I feel some new time around me,
Even though rain still falls from gray-uniformed clouds.
In every youth there are longing glances
For the human body. A coincidence ...
Blanca's eyes are also different.
It seems that other creatures on this planet
Do not have the human taste for pleasure,
As if people came with warm spring rain
And with the timid smell of first primroses.
As if they came from somewhere.
I feel a midnight composition of fear
Instead of faith in the continuity of living.

It seems youth too does not accept boundaries
And instincts rule the planet.

Margitt sends me an e-mail. Around midnight,
When she returns from visiting her neighbors on Bowen Island.
"Do not worry," she writes. "I know you and Norma ...
You worry about the children as if they were alone
In the world.
Blanca is in good hands here.
Mine went somewhere too,
And I was scared of loneliness.
But they returned in a carriage brimming with life.
A carriage awaits her too
And in it some different time.
And the flowers abounding in Eden's nectar
From the Pacific Islands of the North.
Shelley and Bill are good people!
In their house roses bloom always.

Where roses bloom all year round,
There rains are also different."

MY THOUGHTS

My thoughts flutter
Like tree blossoms
Carried by a gentle breeze making flowery snow,
And down the alleys,
Through the turquoise rays of sorrow,
Weaving them into crimson drifts.

They catch me unaware,
As a flower touched by a butterfly
Sparkling the petals' imagination
With the hues of its wings;
As when in the harbor's calm,
In the sails of sleeping vessels,
Sudden waves conjure
Thirst for running,
A dance on water.

They force me to feel
That in the dark middle of night
Rays of light are waiting silent,
That time and space are mysteriously
Entwined in our lives,
As if wanderlust is born
From spindrift long dispersed.

My thoughts are playful
Like baroque facades,

Though for more than hope
I never hoped.

PANORAMA

I couldn't sleep last night,
For no serious reason.
Just a timid trembling feeling.

Irmin came back at five in the morning
From one of his escapades of all-night Vancouver.
And I had worried
For he hadn't returned from his evening shift!

This morning I watched the ashy clouds
Over gray waves of the Pacific Ocean,
Down there, for miles below the windows
Of the mysterious Lady Gem .
The dawn exposed the cracks in the cloudy sky
And there was no sign of my friends from the universe.
In the living room of the affluent ground floor
The friendly poodle Cindy
Touchingly apologized
For disturbing my peace with its yawning.

It is a pleasure to read *V.P.* by the Bosnian poet Izet Sarajlic,
And page after page to ask jealously if the poet stole
My feelings.
He was waking up in this world before I was
And before me was gleaning red apples of life
That moonlight tossed
From large-crowned trees at midnight.

With a handful of crumbling soil,
Ready for the casket of the loved one,
The poet was angry at his friend Viktor Sklowski's thought
That "there is no past and that living hurts."

In the awakened cathode screen
Swings Josh Groben's melody,

Whose voice in the family of tenors
Equals Baroque in Expressionism.

CONTEMPORARY POETRY

In the trembling you're soft, melancholy
Nameless, shapeless
Your eyes like pears
Ripe and juicy
Worm-eaten

She danced on my forehead

In the horse's hairy tail
Her smell
Scattered shadows on the neck
Reddish foam
Silky
To comb, fountain, or chaos alike

From one dog's bark to another
Two long hours
Of carelessness
Behind the brows
Through dreams
Through softness
Sweet tear breaking

Thus audacious you triumphed

Your song was not a lark's
Nor did you chirp in your chirping

In the morning among blades of grass
At noon a rosy prominence
In the whiteness

SEED

In the primeval compass
The heat of the trembling bell
Plunges

Down the lumpy furrow of passion
Like the midnight's sleeping scent
The source moves closer to the mouth
In the desire to return to itself
To crawl back into the mother's womb

Down the dark blue mist
The bulbous-headed lust sinks
Beneath the surface
Its lips distorted

Long
Trembling long
With soft fur around the neck
In the clench of anxiety
The bulbous-headed desire sinks
Beneath the surface

FATE

Is not *fate* proud and mute,
Tortured by difficulty, wrinkled by a rock,
Like rubber stretched by hand,
When returning in dangerous flight?

Is not *fate* somebody's power,
And pride, mad luck,
Stick and arrow,
Bullet and space station;
For some, may the Creator of *fate* forgive me,
Soiled birth into the trash heap?

Isn't *fate* triumph and death
In the eyes of the victor
And in the eyes of the victim?!
That same *fate* in which the flame sparks
And dies ...

Is not *fate* for the spiteful one
Who turns off the light in another man's harbour,
The same as that for the one infected by hate
Whose encomiums sneak back to a suspicious past?!

Is *fate* ashamed of the crystal glasses raised to the sky,
And of the abyss in the eyes of the unfortunate,
And of the newly born orphans
Under the decks of the victor's ships?!

Isn't *fate* like a comet
Whose dusty trail
Batters us across time and space
And pulls a butterfly from cocooning larvae
Before our very eyes?

I SAW

The geese flew over the imaginative tops of skyscrapers
And screamed while flying south,
Where the courage of this frost behind mist fails.
Where the doors to return are open.
Window panes offered me a mirror,
The weary ocean surface offered me wonder.

I saw steaming sparks in my eyes
And the memory of the woman with a rose in her hair
In my pupils.
I saw ... how the gray gloss,
Like the one on the paintings of wisdom,
Conquers the gracious arch of dark brows
And foments melancholy in the bud of surprise.

I saw in my dream the game of her senses.
I dreamed of the wind of awakened scents
Blowing locks of her hair
Above the crimson spring of thrilling purity.
I saw. She is being taken down the road of warmth
Back again into my memory.

I saw her blue eyes
In my dark ones.

Then I saw ... The reddish water has awoken,
The waves' crowns like seagulls.

Fishing boats hastened to the harbor.
The sky in the dark depth of water.
I saw the eclipse of the sun
And the world frightened of darkness at noon.

Behind my back
The screen invited me to watch Michael Moore
Grabbing the ruined statue of Bush Junior
From the hands of angry patriots

And carrying it in his hands
To the graveyard of the great.
To the place of no return
From where the sun never comes.
Beyond the eclipse. Never ...

WOMEN IN MY NIGHTS

The women in the nights of my conquests
Were stronger,
Stubbornly confident when we touched,
Warm and polite,
Playful at the edge of trust,
Offering blue irises to the eyes of passersby.
I crept into their power
With a feeling of hopelessness.

The trembling of their bodies bewilders passion.

They stole the fragrance of their plump bosoms
From my eyes.
On my face they drew smiles.
While I was fighting the boiling breath in my lungs,
They roamed the pages of my innermost feelings.
The women performed the ballet of their hips
On the frozen lake of my wonderment
And threw the boiling balls of powdered snow
At the membrane of shyness
Under my eyelashes.

They are only
snowflakes of mute greetings
in the carriages of my midnight shamelessness.

MAESTRO

The rain came down softly
And sat on a wooden bench
Still warm from lovers' bodies.
Just awakened nocturnal darkness
Attracts rare winged creatures
Under the shimmering warmth of street lamps.

A robbed seagull squeaks on a balcony's fence.

Through the half open window
The smells of sweet dishes in a magical Chinese feast
Bring voices that paint the dilemma
Of the beginning of the new age.
On the cold edge of the untrod pavement
A poor man huddles close to the bare back
Of an equally wary dog.

There,
Beyond the oracular waves of water,
Only two steps away from the street lamps,
Melancholy sounds of violins start calling.

And then,
Over the facades of the surprised city
The raving sounds of a piano
Spill crimson riffs of passion.

It is the mysterious genius
Diving boldly through my tranquil soul
And stealing the mirth of windplay from my eyes.

The notes play a daring pirates' dance,
Dashing boldly through the magic treasure of my past,
And, like torches in the awakened genes of imagination
Create their version of her face.
He penetrates shamefully through the spaces of my egoism,
Rousing feelings in the time of my innocence,
His hands reach for her hair.
Touch the silvery strings of her pride
And then the fingers retreat ashamed
Of their daringness to touch the intimate.

Somewhere
From the Pacific Islands of Haida-Gwaii
The flakes of the late snow start falling
Performing a game of some other life
In front of the astonished eyes of a tiny white puddle.

DESCRIPTION

The blue violet opens its crown
In the sea of hawthorn bushes
With whiteness in their emerald hair.

The yellow breeze passes downhill

Past the murmur of the red chrysanthemums
In the blossoming fire of the sterile quince
The humming of the endless blueness brings dew

The bluish flame of the morning furrows
With the flight of anxious birds
Toward tomorrow's nuptial orgies

Packs of blitzing antennas

To roads murmur adheres
Like a dizzying blue universe
Of extravagant inner awakenings

AN ODE TO WOMAN

You came to me quietly from scented dreams
Like an agile doe
With fear in your eyes.
You approached with suspicion,
Like a wave approaching the cliff.
You feared our love ...

You came to me from another world
Where the imagination of the young men reigns,
You, my rose, with fear in your eyes.

I created your face through cobwebs
Behind closed eyelashes.
As you trembled in the leaf of a delicate willow
You held out your hands to me downwind
And caressed me with your whispers.

You came to me softly from willows by the river,
Like a wave approaching a cliff,
You, my rose, with fear in your eyes.

BEGGAR

Toss me a coin
But softly, please.
In the basket of my silver weaving
Feelings are silent.
Don't roust the dream of the dreaming one.
Whole fields of seeds sleep
In the basket of my silver weaving.

Lay it down gently.
Let it murmur only.
In its song my happiness dreams.
In the midst of our city,
Somewhere under these candles,
My gleaming palace lies hidden
Among massed yellow tulip gardens.
In crimson sleep shadow my yearnings
Empty joy from the ewers of aromatic vines,
And sighs of melancholy breathe life
Into purple fragrant flowers.

Give me a coin
And that only
When your gift bears no silent anger
That I live among the lives of others.
Give,
As from the depth of the sea
A dolphin's play

sprays a salty dew drop to kiss
A blade of grass on an arid rock.

Don't give a lot!
In your coin my hope lives.
If you gave me the riches of the city,
The desire that fuels dreams would die.
Lay it down softly
Lest the ringing metal disrupt my dreams.
I enjoy in dream
The richest life
In the basket of my silver weaving.

LIFE

Life is a congregation of flames in a fire
That burns out and passes away,
And a blade of grass waging fierce battle
To emerge from under the horny soil
And reach for the sun.

Life is like water when,
Conceived by the sun,
It soars toward the azure sky
And when above
In its inspired adventure
Into curious shapes,
Inspirational and horrific,
Transforms,
And to the artist offers its Sistine idea,
And to the sorcerer, predictions
Of the fruits of his sorcery;
And it awakens hope for a fresh drop
In the thirsty blade of grass
And in the withered human creature.

Life is a like a torrent of roiling waters
Just before rampaging into the open sea,
Death of the self in an abyss full of other lives.
Or sometimes hiding under thick blocks of ice
In the liquid of crystal wine glasses
Awaiting its spring.

Life is found in the coarse games of crazy politicians.
It is conceived in deaths,
Regenerating in the bacilli of rotting meat.

Life is the perpetual movement from beginning to end
On the circle of time,

In which each imagined point
After merciless climbing
Into the adventure of certain descent falls.

Life is spewed forth by the volcano's lava.

Undefeated, from the sleeping city
It retreats, from the frozen churchbells
And, like the intoxicating smell of fresh bread,
Life transforms into the games of lives of tomorrow.

MEN AND GOD

Some people have God
To help them on the path to happiness.
Some swear to God till death
As if taking him out of their pockets.
To some God is a hidden hope
For something better when this life ends.
To some he is just a façade
To reach personal goals.

Sometimes God is blamed for sorrows
People encounter on their life paths.
At times they raise his name to the heavens
Or push him into a half-broken vessel.

For him they built mighty and lavish edifices
Filled with darkness and wax candles,
Instead of giving him fields
Adorned with the sun and fragrance of flowers.

Some show him reverence piously and passionately
For all that sets him apart from humans.
For some he is the designer
Who created order on Earth and in the universe.

Some grasp God firmly in their fists,
Waving with him.
And he, perhaps, smiles mysteriously

And casts an eye on my rhymes.

To me is beautiful the old idea
That even the sons of Satan feel
They can wash away their repulsive origins
If they follow God's paths.

THE BLIND WITH THEIR EYES OPEN

How wise
Under the veil of hidden dreams
You are, Pandora, the queen!
In an empty glass imagination reigns.
Paths of ignorance teeming with footsteps.
In my head, the heavy silence
Of the drenched city.

All wait for the miracle when the blind recover their sight.

Antennae in my bosom thread
Crimson contours of consciousness.
Within a political scene of drunken doctors,
Hippocrates
Sees a new arena of human lives,
And changes his will.
Mixed rules in the confusion of madness.
Bodies bind with grass roots ...
Barbarism instead of hope!

In my soul souls murmur:
Pandora in chains!
Gods bound, hallucination ...
Bouquets in broken vases.

The blind dash in with their eyes open.
In the underworld of limp power
Odors sprout.

IF HE EXISTED ...

If he existed,
Would so much pain rumble over this planet,
And would life start in such agony
And fade away in such fear?
Would they,
From the trembling hands of saintly Adem,
In front of his frozen eyes,
Snatch his daughter Samira
And with a blade
Take out her eyes.

If he existed,
Would such mighty human mind
Commit barbarian atrocities against people
And withdraw before the instincts of the insane?
Would it be possible
For a maniac to rule the planet,
And in the strategy of perverse abuse,
The lives of the innocent, the good, and the clever
To account for nothing.

If he existed,
Would the principle of dominance govern evolution,
That merciless way of climbing and devouring,
And would every inch of human progress
Choke in the sea of pain and tears?
Would he create such an order of things

In which profiteers sit on the backs of miners and shepherds
And in which the weapons of the mighty
Dismember the bodies of the weak
On their doorsteps!?

Would he demand that they pray to him on their knees
In dark dwellings,
That they drink human blood in his name,
Leeches,
And that they tyrannize the human soul,
And open the mind to questionable values ?

And that they rejoice when shouting
That the children of nationally mixed parentage are hybrids
And God's creations lacking identity!?

AUTUMN

drop to drop
a river, a fury
of a thousand blue blades
with an icy shriek in its hair

silence in whiteness

bundles of hot sheaves
wailing
amid cracks stone flowers
bawling
above, gossamer chill brings dew

a rumble with bread at its core

across fields an abundant autumn
burns in straw-colored despair
with traces of tears in its eyes

PATHS

In the early morning, I met a breath of sunlight
On its magical journey
Along the path
Beyond our senses,
And I understood the whispering of quinces in blossom
In early spring,
And giggling girls blooming prematurely
Somewhere in the East,
In the fragrant hills of my beginnings.

Somewhere from the East
Fading car-lights enter
My pupils
And go
Towards some still sleeping Western harbors.
Oh, how they rush
From East to West
And nervously wait in front of traffic-lights!
At somebody's words
My thoughts dither,
Recalling David Suzuki's prophesy
That the breath of the sun's light will be ever darker
In our eyes.

Those who go from West to East
Quest by instinct
Through foaming waves to reach the narcotic unknown.

Those others
In the procession
In the opposite direction
Rock on the smooth waves of illusion
And sail over the luminous horizon.

With its magic brush,
The evening sun purpled the snow
On tops of the western mountains
And lured the eyes of curious fishes
Onto the surface of the big water.

Someplace north,
On some frosty island,
A fever gaze of the poet Terry Gucker
Discovered fear in the eyes of ever-warmer glaciers.

Northern lights called on me in the evening
Above Vancouver,
And performed a dance of some strange life
Stolen from my imagination.

In this transition to a new age, as well poets dream
And force some new designs
Into the skillful hands of the seamstresses of our senses.

Third Part

GALACTIC BELONGING IS MORE IMPORTANT TO ME THAN TRIBAL TRADITIONS

HER FACE HAD AN expression of glad tidings when I met her at the Vancouver airport at approximately midnight, five years after the incomprehensibly destructive attack on the New York World Trade Center skyscrapers. Five years after the event that the history of civilization will perennially write about in its Believe It or Not columns. Half a decade had passed since a handful of cave people from the dry desert of the Near East had dealt a heavy destructive blow to the strongest power in the world on its own territory at the beginning of the third millennium after Christ, or Issa Prophet. It was then, using the darkest of methods, that it was proven that the strongest power in the world is not safe, and is surrounded by hatred. This was the only real blow to be dealt America since her foundation. But, not the five years that have passed, nor the encyclopedic recitation of countless facts about people attacking each other; not the news on the Internet that the American occupation forces, forces of destructive revenge, have assisted in the massive plundering of artistic works from Baghdad's libraries and art galleries, the theft and destruction of millions of irreplaceable books and manuscripts from that part of the world known as the cradle of civilization; not the news broadcasts from independent world media stating that, in three years of war in Iraq provoked by the open American-British aggression against the sovereign regime of the dictator Saddam Hussein, more than 650,000 Iraqis had perished, even though Bush Junior insisted that only 50,000 had died ... None of this was more important to me, at the moment when I looked into the mass of travelers, than the mystery of her softly smiling face.

She looked determined. She insisted, with the strength of her exceptional will power, that even though it was after midnight, and even though she had traveled six hours by plane from Honolulu, and in spite of her better than eighty-year age, she was not tired. Her characteristic smile, unlike Mona Lisa's, did not carry in itself the mystery of centuries, but nonetheless did not make known what was hidden in the comet-tail brightness it shone through the weak light of Arrivals. I often felt confused when I tried to define that smile. Lady Gem always escaped my characterizations of her personality. Even now, after who knows how many times, as I re-read my notes about my meeting with her, and her talk with Stephen Hawking in my name, I am in two minds whether or not I should change her nickname in the text for someone else's, for the name of some woman who hadn't wronged me with a cruel injustice. But I won't go there. When I put her kindness toward me on one side of the scale, together with my affection for her, it outweighs the other side, the injustice she once did me. Lady Gem embodies all the good qualities that forever characterize good people. Perhaps that is why I think that in memories one should always nurture acts of kindness and love, and that one should always banish evil and hatred into one of Hawking's black holes, so that they can never return.

"In Honolulu, it took them three hours to discover that the airport scanner had shown an unusually shaped pancreas in a woman's abdomen, and not some kind of hidden mine to blow up the plane," Lady Gem told me as soon as we met, as if she was afraid that she would forget mention this story if our conversation began with the usual greetings. "The world has definitely been overcome with fear of terrorists. It will take decades of following a good, intellectually led path for civilization to recover peace and calm among people."

Lady Gem said this about the subject I had been pondering while I was waiting for her. If I did not know her, I would have added that the American president, Bush Junior, was playing an ugly role, for he had quickened the trend toward world-wide hatred of America, reversing the former sentiment that America was the hope of our civilization. He had accelerated the onset of a future this superpower had in store for itself anyway, because human beings cannot overcome the instinct to dominate and the instinct to conquer when they get hold of power and money. However, I let this comment pass over silently, as I knew that Lady Gem is right-wing, and profit is as important to her as it is to America, and that she thinks hegemony is the best method of survival within earthly circumstances. According to her, I am mistaken in my belief that America could have conquered the world with kindness and not with military force. Everything that I told her when we met and in the car on the way to her home in West Vancouver is unimportant. She, obviously, endeavored to reward my long wait for her at the airport in a way that would make me happy.

"I managed to get hold of Hawking. Stephen is phenomenal. He is a vital intellect. A scientist and prophet whom one should trust. There is no need to wait for centuries to pass so that time will prove his thoughts correct. I felt sorry for him when I caught sight of him and felt the pain of his bodily destitution. So animated in front of me, he seemed like a being fashioned from a small percentage of natural human material and a large percentage of that which humanity has manufactured. But, as soon as we started talking, I stopped feeling sorry for him. I immediately grasped that, although I am physically much bigger than this diminutive person, my larger body stood no chance at all in comparison to his intellect."

On Granville Street our conversation was drowned out by the roaring sirens of two enormous fire engines and several ambulances, which I found increasingly intolerable. I often think that this shrieking of emergency vehicles does more harm to healthy people than it helps those whom they are hurrying to save. At home we were greeted by a small, excited poodle who jumped up at Lady Gem. It is a toy she-poodle named Mine. Lady Gem took out a paper from her small suitcase and, handing it to me, proposed:

"I brought you the Hawaiian Declaration to read. If you're not tired, sit and wait while I change out of these clothes so that I can tell you about Hawking. Mine would like to keep us company."

This was courteous flummery, since Lady Gem knew that her meeting in Honolulu meant much more to me than sleeping, and that the tiny poodle was at least as charming to me as a blanket and, perhaps, ugly dreams. Mine lay down on the couch beside me and looked at the paper in my hand as if to suggest that I read it. The document was more necessary to me than I was to the poodle, so I took up Mine's suggestion. Sometimes in our decisions just one particle of dust turns the balance of our sensibility and uncertainty.

The first sentences of this document at once reminded me of documents of the Organization of Nonaligned Nations. A human attempt with a lot of naiveté! Before long, I blamed my own cynical thoughts, as I began to inhale the heavy and powerful scent of happiness that people had at last decided to extend a definitive hand of welcome to representatives of extraterrestrial civilizations. There are written proofs of visits to our planet by extraterrestrial vehicles from the very beginning of our literacy to today, especially during the period of my life. There have been several times when I myself have had the good fortune to see the flying machines that have visited us. Because of that, the Declaration formulated in the Hawaiian archipelago in 2006 was my document, too. Nonetheless, the truth is that in my opinion it is not precise enough in its characterization of human beings.

To: Citizens of the World
Hawaii Declaration on Peaceful Relations with Extraterrestrial Civilizations

"A New World If You Can Take It"

We, the individuals and institutions participating in and/or supporting the Extraterrestrial Civilizations & World Peace Conference in Kailua-Kona, Hawaii, June 9-11, 2006,

Are a body of concerned private citizens who are promoting world peace and harmonious relations with extraterrestrial civilizations,

Recognizing the overwhelming evidence pointing to the presence of extraterrestrial civilizations, and their generally peaceful interaction with individuals and governmental authorities,

Inspired by the profound significance for humanity of sharing the wisdom, knowledge, culture and technology provided by extraterrestrial civilization.

Asserting that extraterrestrial civilizations have been observing human evolution for some time with particular interest in humanity's quest for lasting peace among its peoples,

Noting that extraterrestrial civilizations have indicated that the abolishment of nuclear weapons worldwide is a necessary milestone toward peaceful coexistence on earth and as a prerequisite for open contact,

Recalling United Nations resolutions concerning international co-operation in the peaceful exploration and use of outer space, banning atmospheric and underwater nuclear tests, and proscribing hostile acts on the moon and other celestial bodies,

Recognizing a range of initiatives promoted by private citizens and citizen organizations with regard to extraterrestrial civilizations visiting Earth,

Intending for this Declaration to be used as a starting point for a greater public dialogue with those holding similar or diverging perspectives and interests concerning extraterrestrial visitation,

Using a consensual decision making process among speakers, organizers, and participants at the Extraterrestrial Civilizations and World Peace Conference, 2006, we have agreed to,

Honor the following principles for establishing peaceful relations with extraterrestrial civilizations:

1. We affirm the intent of humanity to join in peaceful and cooperative relations with extraterrestrial civilizations,

2. Affirm support for United Nations resolutions promoting the peaceful use of Outer Space, and support for UN, International and U.S. Congressional initiatives to prevent an arms race in outer space, including the weaponization of space,

3. Affirm the natural right of all citizens to have open contact with representatives of extraterrestrial civilizations in all cases, and to engage in non-official diplomacy,

4. Declare the need for Civil Society to develop acceptable protocols (standards of behavior) with extraterrestrial civilizations, that the protocols should be representative of the aspirations of all humanity, and that all nations should work in concert to establish peaceful relations,

5. Cooperate with extraterrestrial civilizations in promoting Earth, Cosmic and Life friendly technologies, and encouraging the right use and open availability of these technologies,

6. Affirm our desire to coordinate the earth's ecological health and biological diversity with extraterrestrial civilizations that can aid us in that endeavour,

7. And express our desire to welcome the open appearance of benevolent extraterrestrial civilizations.

"They translated it into hundreds of the world's languages and wrote it in several non-verbal symbologies, with the intention of sending it into space using various methods," Lady Gem said about the text of the Declaration when she appeared in a mildly rose-colored housecoat.

I protested, "It's not sufficiently sincere and does not warn those who come to us from space how dangerous people are. But I think that they are not naïve and that they will not lightly enter into contact with people. In fact, they haven't done this so far because they have enough evidence of our aggressiveness and evil deeds against our own biological kind. It is enough for them to know that in our civilization, from the First World War to the beginning of the third millennium, we have had around 100 smaller and larger wars and that in these approximately 160 million humans have perished, and more than 500 million have been either seriously or slightly wounded. Is there a larger crime or disgrace in our galaxy?"

"Hawking said a similar thing to me. As far as I could grasp it, he is not an optimist when the subject is the open cooperation of extraterrestrial civilizations with us. He weaves everything including God into this, which greatly surprised and disappointed me. Such a mind, which has succeeded in hypothesizing the dimensions of the universe, the beginning and the end of everything, and he gives in to the manipulations of religious institutions." Lady Gem was becoming angry.

"I think he meant that there are forces which arrange relations within the cosmos, and not, literally, a God in the religious sense as it is used here on Earth", I said.

"It's not important. In fact, it is important, but … That is a human disgrace. Stephen is a good proof. Some people are afraid of giving up traditions because they think that they will end up without an identity. My identity is not that which my father left me as an inheritance, but that which I do and choose. For some, conservatism is the very essence of morals. Within the framework of this shell of the past, some feel safe, saved, God-pleasing, as if God, as they imagine him, had not arranged the cosmos so that the previous second has nothing in common with the second that comes after. If there really is anything in the cosmos that is not conservative, then that is God. Suppose that people in their beliefs imagined God in the way Hawking sees cosmos. Then the strictest dogma would be that of perpetual movement and change. Stephen Hawking's studies of the cosmos are an exceptional base and support for a revision of religion."

She searched my eyes, and then winked teasingly, knowing that I knew what she was going to say – because she'd said it so many times before.

"Even I would, perhaps, follow them if they regularly updated their learning. Shall we have a Stolichnaya with cranberry juice?" she asked, plucking at the plumes of Mine's shaggy tail.

Lady Gem both asked the question and decided the answer. And she mixed the drinks herself out of Russian vodka and Canadian juice. As a result of several sips of the drink, she began in a most authoritative tone:

"I know that he prefers to speak about the beginning and the end of the cosmos, about its expansion because of the Big Bang, about black holes and about dwarf stars. In his books, Stephen talks about this as if he's telling a fairy-tale, effortlessly, with lots of imagination, but it is scientifically convincing. On the other hand, he was prepared for other topics too ... He stressed that, while he is a first-class mathematician and physicist, he does not hate any branch of science, as they are all from one enormous orchard that is full of rich realities mixed with intuitive imagination."

She reached out to stroke Mine, but when she saw that the dog had placed its head on my lap and was sleeping, she leisurely withdrew her hand, not wishing to disturb the sleep of her favorite.

"Perhaps it seems crazy to you, but you know my theory is that Hawking cannot be simply a human being and that his beginning came from genes which arrived from somewhere in space, from some abundantly well-developed civilization. And not just his. After all, you are familiar with my thoughts about the great minds of the world," I tried to hurry her along.

"I didn't have the courage to tell him that. Put better, we met for a moment in the courtyard of the building in which the Conference was being held, and Hawking had, it seemed, a very full program of formal official and private engagements. Then, too, that which is human in him has its limits. I would have liked it if you could have met him yourself, in an environment favorable to Stephen, so that there would have been the time and conditions necessary for you to satisfy your curiosity. If I had begun as though I were speaking to someone who associates with extraterrestrials – he might have become angry. If Stephen has the intellect of a being from some other civilization, it is possible that he may not realize it. We, generally, think that we know more about ourselves than others know about us.

I told him that those discoveries of his about black holes were disappointing you. He was silent as if he thought that this was in no way a surprise, but that it was completely normal for those who follow his courageous movement along the roads of science to be disappointed. I explained to him: his theory of black holes is disappointing because following that theory leads to the understanding that there are only black holes – 'The older it is, the more powerful it is.' If so the rest of the cosmic body has a life similar to that on Earth: Be born, grow, flower and create something new, then fall under the process that leads to death, and die. How this happens is not important. In an explosion, or in infinite minimalization. Stephen responded in his metallic voice, which emerged from somewhere inside his digital equipment. He said something like this." She mimicked Hawking's computer-enhanced voice:

s. hawking: Don't you think, dear lady, that each life carries within itself the beginning of that which will end it? If you, like an astrophysicist, become intimately familiar with the processes in space, you will easily see that they are like a comprehensive life system. And every life has a beginning and an ending and, I'll put it this way, a reincarnation. And the cosmos is born in a painful white-hot explosion of violently compacted matter, and then it pulsates. If you ignore time, because one cosmic pulsation is infinite for us, then you will understand that something born of an explosion stretches an elastic membrane around itself, to the extent that the membrane can stretch, and to the extent that pressure can be exerted on it, and then, when the power of the beginning explosion becomes weaker than the strength of the elastic power of the membrane, this membrane, as it is elastic, compresses back that which the explosion had expanded. And then it happens all over again, because time and space are infinite. Behind every unit of time stands the next, and behind every enclosure in space there exists another.

"So what, then, about life, and living material in the cosmos?" I asked.

So you think that the Earth is a cosmic peculiarity?! he said, looking like a surprised teacher. Then he went on:

s. hawking: The cosmos is composed of a definite number of chemical elements. And in the cosmos, as within us, hydrogen dominates, but it would not mean anything in the formation of life without the processes with which other elements are formed. Temperature, pressures and explosions are the greatest creators in the cosmos. In the explosion of mega stars, for instance, life begins. In this process, light metals such as carbon and oxygen are created. There, where the temperatures and concentrations of elements provide good conditions for the formation of cells and molecules, is where life is born and grows. Just as up to now in our civilization, from huge catastrophes, such as wars, a period of unprecedented development of new things is emerging. For us neighbors in the cosmos are hugely remote from each other, so it is impossible to throw a rock from one courtyard into another. Because of that, the majority of people believe that we are alone in the universe.

"And are we alone?" I asked him as a student would ask a teacher.

s. hawking: Today many people know that we are not alone. Not long ago, scientists at Berkley University in California proved that organic molecules that travel about the universe in comets can survive their contact with the Earth and sow various forms of life upon our planet. And they arrive from some universal oases of life. My friends Wickramasingh and Hoyle have scientifically proven that clouds between stars within our galaxy are full of bacteria cells that carry within themselves the genetic information necessary for the formation of various types of living organisms. From these clouds, stars, planets and comets are formed. Comets transport this living material around the cosmos. To planets, for instance, such as Earth. Every day, approximately one hundred tons of debris from comets falls on the Earth. This cosmic detritus brings us various types of bacteria, which have a substantial influence on life on our planet. In 1996, NASA confirmed that fossilized bacteria had been found in a piece of a meteorite from Mars.

"And intellectual life in space? I tried to provoke him. *Today this is being written about more than ever before,* I tried to direct him towards that which interests us more than anything else. I was unsuccessful. He avoided answering, perhaps because many of the Conference participants were seeking to have him speak about this. He said only that, so far, Kepler, Galileo, Newton and Darwin had maintained that life is not a phenomenon unique to Earth. For his part, Darwin had developed his understanding of biophysics to a cosmic extent in which the human being is a part of a much larger chain of life, not simply the top of a chain of human-like monkeys on Earth. I was interested in Stephen's thoughts about Tesla, so I mentioned that even a hundred years ago that Croatian Serb physicist was sure other intelligent beings exist in the cosmos, and that he had created a radio-system for communicating with extraterrestrial civilizations. Hawking looked more and more nervous, though sitting so still in his wheelchair. He reminded me that my late husband had harboured thoughts of sending TV pictures into space with information about life on Earth and with welcoming greetings to members of other civilizations."

"Why are you asking me about what you already know?" he said in the end. "I have not met anyone who was not from our civilization. But, at this Conference, there are many people who have. Either beings or their flying craft. Try to talk about that with American presidents, with the Pope and his cardinals ..."

"I noticed that somebody was looking intently at us, or more to the point, at Stephen – a man dressed in clothing that you could say was traditionally English. He came up to us and wiped beads of sweat from Stephen's forehead. Hawking looked into my eyes, nodded his head as a sign that the interview was ended and turned his small, moveable table towards a corner of the auditorium that was dominated by coconut palms. Jeanne was charmed by my story when I spoke to her about Stephen later, in the Honolulu Airport. John and Ron, too."

Lady Gem once again made her version of the well-known drink, with a lot more vodka and less juice, and pulled her armchair closer to me and Mine. It was as if the alcoholic flavor was agitating intimacy in her.

"You're the one who is responsible for my feeling that this cosmic enigma presses heavily on me like a frozen wind from Alaska. Pat Quinn helped your argument with his talk of balls of light that followed him across the plains of Ontario; they weren't helicopters, cars or lights in people's hands. But you infected me with your news of unidentified flying objects in the skies of Ukraine, Bosnia and over Vancouver. Now, it is amazing to me that I did not know earlier about the drawings, thousands of years old, of cosmic people with antennas on their heads, that were found on the walls of Australian caves. I didn't know that over six thousand years ago the Sumerians wrote of extraterrestrials who came from Mars, others from the Pleiades, and still others from planets of Sirius, so long ago, and they knew what the Solar system looks like! And then, like the Sumerians, even though contact with Sumer was impossible, four thousand years ago the members of the Inca civilization in South America wrote that they knew that the world is round and that gods came from the Pleiades."

Lady Gem paused and looked at me so suggestively that I knew that it was necessary for me to say something on this theme, whether it was something new or something repeated for the umpteenth time. No matter how many times I talked to her about my knowledge of extraterrestrials, she reacted as if she was listening to it for the first time.

"You haven't forgotten about the scrivener of the pharaoh Tutankhamen the Third, who wrote that in the 22nd year in the third month of winter, a fiery ball arrived from the sky, that the pharaoh in a panic ordered soldiers to surround him, but that the ball took again back up to the sky. Then, the troops of Alexander the Great, 329 years before the modern era, were attacked by two flying objects. And there is much other written evidence proving visits by extraterrestrials to Earth. In 1716, the British astronomer Halley announced that he had seen a series of unexplainable flying objects, and in 1947 an extraterrestrial craft crash landed in America, at Roswell, New Mexico. That same year a businessman and pilot from Idaho in America reported that in the vicinity of Mount Rainier, just below Seattle in the north-western United States, he saw a formation of nine silver-colored objects flying at tremendous speed," was my short report of some facts regarding extraterrestrials' presence on our planet.

"It amazes me why the Americans have not reported their state secrets about UFOs," Lady Gem reflected out loud.

"Their secrets have begun to escape," I said. "You know, the US Air Force Academy confirmed that our planet is visited by extraterrestrials, and that they are from three, or four different civilizations at various stages of development. The former American president Jimmy Carter promised his voters that he would open the government secret files connected with UFOs, but that he was forbidden to do so by the then director of the CIA, George H.W. Bush, Junior's father."

"I have read your series of poems '*I Know That We Are Not Alone*' ten times. This is the first poetry that talks about relations with extraterrestrials that I have read. They don't even give you peace in poetry!"

"I have always wanted contact with intellectual beings outside our civilization. I never doubted that they exist. Even when I was young, I asked them to show me if they could help so that people would change and become peaceful beings. There, from where I came from, in the Balkans, there isn't a generation that hasn't been befallen by war, killings of people, and the destruction of that which people have built between wars. At night, stretched out under a quilt, I would beg them to produce a virus that would expel aggression and egoism from people, but my mother would pull the quilt off my head and ask what I was whispering underneath it. I would hide behind the stable and with my hands send signals to the sky. I waited for years for an answer. I asked them to help me so that we could guarantee a noble galactic descent for human beings, insisted on our right to have a much better and equal position of friendship, for the severance of our social and cultural isolation, and for the elimination of barriers which hold back our possibilities, interests and responsibilities within the Earth's borders. Perpetually burdened by the bloody history of human beings, their aggressiveness which goes all the way to cannibalism, their lustfulness that goes all the way to tyranny, exploitation and incest, their preference for their own interests to the detriment of society's, I begged those in the cosmos who are not burdened by this to help us so that we could resolve this evil within ourselves. And today I believe that civilization would become more coherent if extraterrestrial civilizations were accepted as fact by everyone. When I began writing, I began to make contact with extraterrestrials real in my work. I am unsure if this instinct to make contact announced itself spontaneously in order that I could help people and save my family and my friends from being killed in some new war, or if something outside the Earth's borders influenced me so that my invitations extended into the cosmos were bringing replies. It was then, when I felt my mind's maturity had arrived, just as in the mountains as soon as the snow melts we feel in the air that it is springtime already behind the first southern peaks, that was when I started to see their flying craft and to feel their presence."

"I know that they exist," Lady Gem said to me in a tone of confession. "Lately I have begun to feel their presence. It seems to me that this contact can be felt by those who believe in them. If I met them, I would beg them to show me if reincarnation is possible. I love life and am happiest when I catch myself dreaming that life has no ending. I'm sorry that I didn't ask Stephen Hawking if, perhaps, black holes are only funnels through which our spirits pass on the way to some other world. Your poem 'Earth's Slaves' encouraged me. If you are to be believed, if our life on this planet is simply a serving out of certain obligations, or punishments, and if we are to return to where we came from, then I am happy in this ending of obligations and punishment. I am not joking and am not under the influence of your poetic creations. I would like to meet them so that I could ask them . They have to know." Lady Gem divulged her belief sincerely as she opened the door with the apparent intention of going up to her bedroom.

I know her well. I know that for her the two glasses of vodka and juice could not have caused her to become confused. And I know that during her entire life, she has behaved completely differently from the way poets do in their poetical worlds. I was genuinely happy with my meeting with Lady Gem that night, and as she walked off up the stairs, I called after her:

"You still have lots of time. You will live for sure for at least another twelve years, and by that time the mission of the huge spaceship from Alpha Centauri into our Solar System will have been completed."

I put the little poodle Mine into her sleeping basket and went into the basement, where my family was living. Norma and Blanca were sleeping on Blanca's bed, and Irmin was in his room in front of a slightly opened window. My oldest son Minko and his family were sinking into night time high up in the north of British Columbia, and the younger one, Iris, was still, certainly being beamed upon by the morning sun, far away on the Balkan Peninsula. My brother Hajro and sisters Semira and Jasna were in America; brothers Fehro and Avdo, and my 88 year old father, in Sweden; sister Selveta in Germany, our legendary Rasid in Bosnia ... Lady Gem, I am sure, could not fall asleep for a long time. She, a famous Canadian Lady, a Vancouver legend, rich and pampered, had given shelter to us, Bosnian war refugees, under the roof of her residence in the best city in the world.

I could not fall asleep for a long time myself that night. I was tormented by my poem "Failing to Describe Pain", which I hade been altering for days, searching for adequate words to describe this state of the human psyche. The world is, in addition to other things, a planet of pain. If there existed a measurement of pain, as could be named *Bosnia* or *Iraq*, it would be difficult to find the mathematical capabilities to measure the collective world pain compacted into one small unit of time. All the pain of those who die, or of those who are heartlessly tortured or killed by others, or of those who know that someone is torturing one of their loved ones, the pain of anyone of the human race, the pain in general existing in nature on this planet. Regardless of the faith that you belong to, it is difficult to grasp the thought that such relations on Earth as *devour or be devoured,* or *kill to profit,* could have been devised by a Creator who has charitable feelings, a Creator who wears a halo of *goodness.* Therefore I often find myself with the blasphemous thought that I cannot thank such a *Creator.* I would be happier to extol people if they were to organize their feelings and minds to do only good. I become alarmed when I find myself thinking that the world is just one tiny part of the cosmos and that she is ruled by cosmic rules. Because, in this boundless movement of matter from one empty space into another, this creation by violent explosion, and on the basis of the destruction of what went before, there exist other civilizations. Do "Earthly" relations exist there, relations full of pain? Hopefully, they do not. Perhaps those beings, they who have developed a much greater degree of perception than ours, have thrown away the process of *devour or be devoured,* and perhaps they really could help us so that each human being would adopt responsibility for all of civilization, for human coherence, so that in human feelings, compassion would become the ruler.

The Sun is one of the young stars in our galaxy, and so too is life in our system younger than those that have developed within the framework of older solar systems. Perhaps this Earthly youthfulness, which is always unruly and unmanageable, will give way to a mature period, when reason will become more rational, and aggressiveness and greed will be tamed. For that to happen, it would be good if some excellent teachers arrived from somewhere to teach us life and behavior worthy of highly intelligent beings in the universe.

THE ALTERNATIVE

A gift came from beyond the reach of my hopes.
From the alternative:
I did not feel time.
In my moments were
The moments of my playing with eternity.

My eyes suggested evanescence.
Images in the eyes.
In memory
The primordial emptiness.
But in a dream my perverse
Desire for innocence
Dives toward its the unreachable boundary.

I yearned for the feeling of existence
And conceived of winning in the lottery of morals.
Pain in the shade of imagined continuity,
The trembling of pride in the swollen bowl of love.

Instead of life
Paraphrases
In my spread arms.
The darkness of the universe in the sea's of glitter,
And frost in the orgies of heat.
Distance.
Even when my frantic spasm
Encircles the blooming buds of my roots,

The primordial bang separates.
And when, exalted after a victory,
I recognize the end of time and space,
A new thought brings me the awareness of infinity.

EARTH'S SLAVES

For this one, the rain has tainted his reason
And woken the sleeping chrysanthemums.
A sea of tiny drops has fallen on his hope
And this morning's trouble frightened him.

For another one, the crystal dew
Has torn the green buds from their stems
And frozen the hot fruits in his heart.

Some king offered his kingdom
For a spavined horse;
For some the glitter of the white palace
Meant more than human lives.

We are never a true whole,
Not even before that fateful birth.
Within us sprouts the magic of evil,
The seeds of turbulent headless destruction.

We are only slaves on Earth,
Trapped in our bodies,
Laden by thought.
Our chains are   gravity,
Our connections – prostitution.

POWERLESSNESS OF THE POWERFUL

Kings are not clowns.
The great embody the power of time
Hidden in patinas of age.
Also when they are cruel, monstrous and hateful,
In their names are the piecework of history.

Pride is here more important than life,
Dignity before the desire to live.

Seventy times Oryana has turned
Into the flower of birth
And to the people of the heights of the Andes
Delivered seventy chosen ones,
Then, when the Moon blushed in embarrassment,
She disappeared into the intricate paths of the universe.

In the midst of the pharaoh's glory,
His naïve youth pushed Tutankamen into
The journey to the unknown,
And some fake poor   -amen
Was wrapped in the eternal clothes
Of the king of the scorching dunes,
And only the graves of cosmic outcasts
Now defy the destructive rage of time.

The whole Mongolian mystery was created
In a test tube with a mystical potion
For the great Khan
Stolen from the vessel
That in the time of the crescent moon
Returned to the blue heights.

At the dawn of the third millennium,
One great nation followed the blind man,

And some strange weakness
Came upon the arms stretched toward the sky
To meet the mystical vessels of hope.

Mysteries wander through human time.
They hide in the ancient mummies.
Holy books are also doctrines of aggression,
As if man were not first man
And then a link in the tribal chain.

Here in the absurd, centuries pass.

MYSTERY

Odin disappeared from the Viking decks
In the spring,
When the scented icebergs arrived from the north
And tore the ropes in the Nordic harbors.
The waters have risen in rivers,
From source to mouth.
The winds have stripped the mountaintops
And lifted masses of snow into the clouds.
The roots,
Like a windswept maiden's hair,
Have risen to the sky and suffocated the treetops.
Large herds of caribou
Fled from human settlements,
Wolf packs hid in their lairs.

A red light has passed through the sky
And disappeared in the fog of the Milky Way.

Someone's ships have seen the west coast of the Atlantic,
And shed blood at the feet of the gorgeous pyramids,
And the dark blue water opened
To release a seductive light,
And dragged the ships into the depth,
Into the unknown …

Later on in Tunguzia, on the West Siberian plains,
On a warm noon day,

Some new sun appeared,
And disappeared into the earth,
Giving rise to hot winds
That burned down the nomads' tents
All the way below Mongolia's borders.
The pharaohs disappeared in mystical tombs
And left behind the gods of the hot sand.
The Greek Zeus sailed away through the Atlantic Gate
With an entire entourage of powerful gods,
While the Roman Bacchus,
Intoxicated with wine,
Fell asleep in the damp catacombs.

The Incas and the Mayans built landing strips
For the arrival of the gods,
While The God began appearing around Jerusalem,
As if the rest of Earth had disappeared in a flood.
Each of his appearances created a new religion,
As if human beliefs mattered to him!

A gray old man waited out these ages
Under a scented linden tree
And his lips repeated the mystery:
"Is God toying with humans,
or are humans toying with God?"

INSIGHT

I was pushed into a body
That the law of transience bends
Where, against my nature,
A countless multitude of lives develops.
I was given this body's shameless eyes to watch
As he, in the phases of the moon,
Drags himself up to the abyss
So that I, in the absence of the measure of eternity,
Admire him in his phases of ascent,
So that in his loneliness,
When I feel that our destiny is tied,
I tremble in fear of his disappearance.

I keep forgetting,
With goblets of passion and imagination,
That it's only my cave:
Through its cracks light penetrates;
It is made of silence
And the silent force of chains:
That his transience forced me into
Dreaming of different relationships.

Time contains the trembling of his roots.

If I were born in him,
My hope would smolder
Encased in eternal wondering.

IN SOMEBODY'S ARMS

I don't know who you really are.
My contact with you has always
Ripped apart my thinking.
Are they yours,
Or mine,
My mystical wanderings,
And have you, perhaps,
Breathed in me
Since I was conceived?

You grow when I feel weak,
Smiling.
Through the abyss of my despair
You smuggle hope.
I am positive
That in the fists of my doubts
I'm not alone.

Even when we,
In the protesting game of time,
Have lost each other,
Through the genetic trail of the tears
On my face
You were borne again
And in the silvery web of wind in my hair
You were whispering your enigmatic meaning.

I feel you adjusting my thought
That negated me into the absurd,
The sobbing of the wounded roots.
In the genetics of my past,
You are wondering over
The barren flaccidity of a eunuch
In the swelling strength of creation.

In sodden dreams,
In the guts of the Trojan horse,
You push me through the aching membrane of a virgin.

Across fallen bridges you begin.

You can't have my feeling of joy
At the images in the depths behind my eyes
You are of a different past.
Your thoughts carry the fragrance of distant places
And the wondering over Darwin's truth
Of spontaneous growth.
Amidst the triumph of my instincts
You shamelessly whisper in my ear
Your version of my beginning.
Sarcastic
In my harmony,
Stubbornly didactic
In my agony.

CHAOS

In that one of long ago,
In the chaos before the beginning,
The seeds of all time sprouted.

In our chaos,
In the one brought to our genes through memory,
In that one are the beginnings of our thinking,
And constitution,
Individualities unskillfully colored.

Then came destructive canons,
And deities,
And faceless forces
Without senses to feel pain.
So chaos crept into the soul's depth,
And its fires holed up in the crevices of our mind,
In shadows.

And then,
Human mind rose above roofs,
And frozen lakes melted,
And the spirit scattered in the universe
As the hope for renewal spread
Through the innards of dead palm-trees,
Like light
Coming through clouds
Creating a silver lining,

And opening paths from that darkness in the depth
To those challenges in the heights.

And the chaos got excited
And became stronger,
Like corn in the field
Coating the kernel with the silk from its bosom,
New oases of chaos in the eternal philosophy of motion.
Chaos instead of a refrain
In the melodies of our reincarnations,
In the continuity of our ascent
And the silent force of time
Drove clumps of that chaos,
The one ripened before the beginning,
Into my hope,
Into the feeling of serenity and warmth.

DREAM

At the corner,
Where two streets touch,
Blossoms the triumph of modern architecture.
On its street level
A beauty with slanted eyes sells straw hats
And silken Cantonese kerchiefs
For inviting women's bosoms.
Up,
Dauntingly high up,
On the fifty-fifth floor,
The sun euphorically crashes itself
Into the mute windows.
A passionate beauty slips out
Of her salacious clothes
And recoils from the smell of somebody's hands
On her breasts.

A constellation of foggy balls
In firm geometrical formation
Levitated off the high seas
Into the mysterious heights of the universe.

Unchecked, the echo
Of the magic word *countdown* steals in
And makes everything on both streets still,
Like a Bill Hoopes canvas,
And menacingly cold

As the time when the roof over an ice rink
Falls upon frozen statues of hockey players,
And in a dreamlike explosion
Turns everything into cubes of ice
For somebody's royal feast.

At another corner people stream at shop windows,
The flash and blare of never-ending sales.
Others vacantly stare at TV screens,
The terrible commercials surging out,
Crass and immoral,
With miracle messages for personality destruction:
This capsule
Guarantees your future happiness!
And at 19.99 it's almost free!!
Our number is nine times zero!
Call now!

Up there,
On the trodden English grass around the Museum of Art,
Hollywood beauties
With artificial breasts and bums
Are shooting a movie about the immense importance of profit
And, with pictures of Nostradamus's pierced eyes,
Stir up fear in the gaze of a Bosnian boy.

HYACINTH

A disembodied face
In the fog of emptiness
Unexpected

With its head under a rock
In the endless gray
Of dawn

Its enraptured mane
Flame of the soil
Engraved

Without a murmur protrudes
The dark blue spring
Of hope

SPOKEN AS A STRANGER

People, I don't want to have features,
Nor to carry a void in the keg of happiness.
I step away from your euphoria
And hide from its Dardanian gifts.

It is your nature
To color entire kingdoms of misery with smiles,
Where fists push bundles of cut flowers,
Dream-tellers erase morale,
Whims change sports T-shirts.

Your eyes symbolise storm clouds,
In your ears rings the music of anger.
I don't want your blood in my veins,
That destructive warmth,
Nor your heart my heart to pull out,
Nor the hope in your dreams!
Nor the atmosphere of stiff smells …
Hope is here the offspring of trouble.

Your caresses are not for love!
Your lips are make-up in front of burning jaws!
Your happiness is Trojan naïve
In the colorful palette of illusion.
You make intrigues on the trail of Zion's commandments.
Who dyed your Easter eggs?
And whose return do you pray for?!

Who are your creators,
From what time?

Fortunately,
From different matter you are coined.
Our genes are different.

BEYOND THE BOUNDARY OF INSIGHT

My world is void of time zones,
And of silence expanding into infinity.
There live faint memories
Of my own membrane of gladness, of sadness
That plunge my heart into the cages
Of imaginative pigeon keepers.
In my world birds have flown beyond the boundary of insight
And discovered the hasty river of the dreamed future.

Mountain tops under the blades of a new day.

I believed that the wisdom of the world
Lay within the thresholds of ancestral homes
And in those timid woods
From which foxes dash after naïve chickens
And ravens angrily grudge at weary dogs
In front of a carriage on the skates of evanescence.
The Wosks show me their roots
Hidden deep in somebody's land.

In my dreams the crimson feeling of insight.

I pursued the traces of moonlight to the book of creation
And searched for the one who moves planetary tides
In eyes that merrily go downwind.

I saw time in album pictures
And on newly frescoed walls.
Blanca and Una
Throw pebbles into the Capilano River.
The Iris and Dino are calling us from across the water.
Unease creeps from afar. Time and wonder.
Drinks make dew on the flush
Under our closed eyelashes.

AT THE GATE OF DEPARTURE

"Your mission is coming to the end,"
He tells me
And a strange smell spreads through my memory.
As if I dreamt it.
"You have paid your debt."

"I think it is not the right time,"
I say.
I let my roots grow in the crystal solitude.
And feelings in the spring wind …
That you can measure neither with instruments,
Nor with time.
This smell is also borrowed from somewhere,
Some time.
And that I am here to pay my debt:
That too!

"Your path is not behind your back,"
He says,
And that smell grows stronger
Reminding of ripe quinces,
Like light becoming stronger
When the sun breaks the night.
I feel everything merciless
And feel pain because of happiness
When I hold it in my arms.

Can I leave without a great pain,
Tell me,
Without leaving pain as my legacy?
Speak ... Tell me!
Without leaving pain at the gate of my departure!

HIDDEN DIMENSION

two lines
parallel
like a frozen memory
akin
like times unlived
stiff
like run-over puppies
laboring to unearth a path
and nothing ever returned to beginning

two lines
frozen
bound to eternity
to blue infinity
and nothing ever returned
to memory

resembling long-vanished
conveyances levitated carriages
in the storm of distrust
or somebody's rinsed-out dream
in my eyes
or another enchanted world
I can not capture in my aching thoughts

and there must be something therein
within

an unfinished image
of someone departing
into an unknown warp of space

ENDNOTES

Isaac Asimov was an American scientist and writer who produced over 500 books that enlightened, entertained and spanned the realm of human knowledge. He was one of the central figures of science fiction for five decades of the 20th century. His breakthrough work, "Nightfall", is acclaimed as the best science fiction story ever written.

Bosnian Krajina is a region in northwestern Bosnia, on the border with Croatia. In the city Bihac, the major center of that region, Tito created the first Yugoslavian Government in 1942, during the Second World War.

George H.W. Bush is a former American President, former Director of the CIA, and father of President George W. Bush, creator of the doctrine of permanent war against terrorists. As Director of the CIA, he forbade American President Jimmy Carter to open the American secret UFO files, citing national security concerns and the need to avoid public panic.

Nicolae Ceausescu was the Romanian dictator during the time of communism. At the end of his power, Romanian revolutionists held a two-hour "kangaroo court" trial and sentenced him, together with his wife, to death by firing squad.

Noam Chomsky is an American linguist, philosopher, political activist, author and lecturer. Already renowned for his theory of trans-formational grammar, beginning with his critique of the Vietnam War in the 1960s he became more widely known for his political activism, in particular his criticism of the foreign policy of the USA and some other governments. Critical of the American capitalist system and big business, he describes himself as a libertarian socialist. In many of his books and articles, Chomsky attacks the double standards of US foreign policy: preaching democracy and freedom for all, while promoting, supporting and allying itself with non-democratic and re-pressive organizations and states. He argues that this results in human rights violations which fit the standard description of terrorism.

Jacques-Yves Cousteau, co-inventor of the AquaLung, pio-neered and popularized oceanographic research with the aim of pro-moting sound ecological practices long before "environmentalism" became fashionable. His research vessel, *Calypso,* was originally a wooden-hulled minesweeper built for the British Royal Navy. The Irish millionaire Thomas Loel Guinness bought *Calypso* and leased it to Cousteau for a symbolic one franc a year. The Cousteau Society continues his work.

Chenrezig: According to Tibetan legend, Chenrezig made a vow that he would not rest until he had liberated all the beings in all the realms of suffering. Tibetan Buddhists believe whenever we are com-passionate, or feel love for anyone, or for an animal or some other constituent of the natural world, we experience a taste of our own natural connection with Chenrezig. They view each Dalai Lama as a reincarnation of this legendary monk.

Erich Von Daniken was born in Switzerland, educated in Germany and became famous – and controversial – in the USA and later in the entire world as the "father of the ancient astronaut the-ory". His first book, *Chariots of the Gods,* popularized the concept of extraterrestrial influence on human civilization.

Erasmus of Rotterdam was a Dutch humanist, writer, philoso-pher and theologian in the time of the Renaissance. After the dark, incredibly tyrannic domination of Christian religious institutions during the Middle Ages, Erasmus helped initiate and supported the reform of Christianity and reawakening of the sciences. His book *The Praise of Folly* (*Encomium Moriae,* in Latin) was small but, at the same time, rich and powerful – disruptive for arrogant religion institutions, inspiring for the new wave of artists, like Dante Alighieri, author of *The Divine Comedy.*

Goya's *Nude Maya* was shrouded in mystery from its first days. The great Spanish artist Francisco Goya painted two Mayas. The *Nude Maya* is probably the most famous nude painting in art history. In the same room with it was a clothed version of the same figure, the *Clothed Maya.* Speculation has it that the nude version used to be hidden behind the clothed version in the same picture frame, and that the lady was the Duchess of Alba, with whom Goya was infatuated. How he managed to get a noble woman to pose this way in Spain at that time is only one of the many mysteries surrounding this work.

Goli Otok (Barren Island) is a small, barren island off the north coast of Croatia. Throughout World War I, Austria-Hungary sent Russian prisoners of war from the Eastern Front to Goli Otok. After the Tito-Stalin split, Goli Otok became a high-security, top secret detention and labor camp for persons imprisoned as Soviet sympathizers. In his 1984 book *Goli Otok – The Island of Death,* Macedonian poet Venko Markovski described the horrors of that prison for the first time. Rifet Bahtijaragic in his novel *Blood in the Eyes* mentions Goli Otok as a grotesque error of Tito's regime.

Mikhail Gorbachev was the last Secretary of the Communist Party of the Soviet Union. His attempt at reform – perestroika – ended the political supremacy of the Communist Party of the USSR and contributed to the end of the Cold War. He has expressed pantheistic views as his religion, saying "Nature is my god."

Okanagan: In the summer of 2003 massive forest fires facilitated by climate change and dubious forest practices destroyed large areas of this British Columbia valley, threatening the city

of Kelowna while consuming many homes and huge tracts of timber.

Publius Aelius Traianus Hadrian was emperor of Rome from 117 to 138 AD. Hadrian was both a Stoic and an Epicurean philosopher. He rejected Christianity as the official religion of the Roman Empire because he didn't want one dogmatic vision of a transcendent God to supplant the many anthropomorphic Greaco-Roman gods. The most illuminating view of Hadrian in our modern era is Marguerite Yourcenar's novel *Memoirs of Hadrian.*

Haida-Gwaii: The archipelago off the northwest coast of British Columbia known to European cartography as the Queen Charlotte Islands. Its name means "Islands of the People," and it is the homeland of the Haida Nation.

Immanuel Kant was a German philosopher, one of the most influential thinkers of modern Europe, one of the most important figures in philosophy after Aristotle. But in his hometown of Konigsberg, people remember Kant for his very strict and predictable life. His neighbors would set their clocks by his daily walks: he got up at five a.m., and after a cup of tea and a pipe of tobacco worked till nine, when he went to lecture until one. He never married

Mostar is a beautiful old city in Bosnia-Herzegovina. The city's symbol, the "Old Bridge" (*Stari Most*), was one of the most important structures of the Ottoman era, built by Mimar Hayrettin. During the last Bosnian War, even though the bridge was under the protection of UNESCO, Croatian forces in Bosnia-Herzegovina destroyed the monument. After the war, the bridge was reconstructed, but without the previous charm of Medieval art and its five-hundred-year-old patina.

John Forbes Nash is an American mathematician, receiver of the Nobel Prize in Economic Sciences. After the movie *A Beautiful Mind,* where the actor Russell Crow presented Nash's very complex, troubled scientific and mystical mind, Nash became well-known throughout the world. A schizophrenic, Nash invented mathematical statements which could perhaps not have been devised without his special, abnormal mind.

Narcissus: In Greek legend, young Ameinias loved Narcissus but was scorned. As a way of rebuffing Ameinias, Narcissus gave him a sword, which Ameinias used to kill himself on Narcissus' doorstep; he prayed that Narcissus would one day known the pain of unrequited love. This curse was fulfilled when Narcissus became entranced by his own reflection in a pool and tried to seduce the beautiful boy, not realizing it was himself. He only realized that it was his reflection after trying to kiss it, and Narcissus took his own sword and killed himself. His body then turned into a flower.

Oryana: Pre-Incan legend asserts that a golden ship came from the stars; in it came a woman, whose name was Oryana. She had only four fingers on each hand. Great Mother Oryana gave birth to 70 Earth children, then she returned to the stars.

Pandora: According to Greek mythology, jealous of Prometheus's exceptional work regarding the creation of human beings, Zeus, the chief Olympic god, created a woman named Pandora. She was as foolish as she was alluring. Zeus sent her to Earth carrying a pot (Pandora's box) that she was ordered never to open. The men, enchanted by her charm, welcomed her among them. But soon, stupidly, she opened the secret vessel, as Zeus knew she would, and out of it flew the miseries that afflict humanity to this day – war, famine, sickness, evil and sin. Only hope, ever deceptive, remained in the pot, a slight comfort.

Bill Reid was a Canadian jeweler, sculptor and artist. He took from his European-descent father a very developed sense for exploring, and from his Haida mother, exceptional artistic vision. In ill health, suffering from almost complete paralysis, he drew "The Hunchback of Haida-Gwaii" on the flyleaf of little girl Blanca Bach's book *The Hunchback of Notre Dame de Paris*. Bill did this in front of his sculpture *The Spirit of Haida Gwaii* at the Vancouver Airport three months before he died.

Revisionism: A deviation from revolutionary Marxian socialism, an evolutionary rather then revolutionary spirit. In the Communist world, the most notorious instance was Tito's Yugoslavian revisionism. This was a deviation from Marx and Lenin's principles of society governed by the *dictatorship* of the proletariat, which in practice meant the dictatorship of the Communist Party. Instead, Tito's Yugoslavia practised the principle of self-governed socialism: the power of workers exercised in a direct self-governing form of democracy with the purpose of achieving material well-being.

Theutus According to Renaissance magician Cornelius Agrippa, Theutus was a demon who taught mankind "all the wicked arts and sciences of warfare, black magic and adornment".

Marshal Tito was baptized Josip Broz. In the year 1941, early in World War II, when the Nazi's and Fascists were taking Europe and Africa part by part, Tito stepped before the Yugoslavian nations and sent a message to the Hitler/Mussolini Axis: "Better war then a pact! Better the grave than becoming a slave!". As President of the Socialist Federal Republic of Yugoslavia, he sent a similar message to Stalin in 1947, and inaugurated the Yugoslav revision of communist ideology. This was the man who created the Movement of Nonaligned Nations together with the Prime Minister of India, Jawaharlal Nehru, and the President of Egypt, Gamal Abdel Nasser. His funeral was the most magnificent of the post-war period. He inspired both Mikhail Gorbachev and the Dalai Lama. Josip Broz acquired the name Tito in primary school, when he would assist the teacher and give direction to his fellow students: "*Ti to, ti to …* " ("Do that, do that …").

Stefan Zweig was a famous Austrian writer, journalist and biographer. Much before today's European Union, he advocated the unification of Europe. He lived in two extreme periods of civilization. After World War I, the Austro-Hungarian Empire disappeared, and in Europe there started to blossom cosmopolitan multiculturalism and tolerance. Jews, Catholics, Serbs, Prussians, Muslims, Gypsies and numerous other peoples mingled and lived in something close to harmony. But nothing good ever lasts, it seems. The Austro-Hungarian Empire splintered and then vanished into the National Socialist hell of Hitler and Mussolini's expanding ambitions. Zweig, one of the most popular writers in the world at that time, together with his wife, committed suicide somewhere in South America's wide spaces.

ABOUT THE AUTHOR

Rifet Bahtijaragic originated in the Balkan Peninsula. Here cultures of East and West mixed, and here also the sectarian politics of power and predominance bred confrontation and ignited destructive wars at least twice during one human's life. Running from that destructive Balkan syndrome, Bahtijaragic has spent the course of his life searching for paths throughout narrow nationalistic and intolerant religious societies close to home and far away and tried to grow into an Earthling with the sensibility of cosmic belonging. In the last war of bloodthirsty nationalisms in Bosnia, he could very easily have been murdered because of his pacifist orientation.

He was born on 7 January 1946 in the small mountain town of Bosanski Petrovac, close to the Croatian border. He finished his university studies fourteen years before the Sarajevo Winter Olympic Games, and during those years worked in two separate fields: as a specialist in economic development for state banks and companies, to make his daily bread; and as a writer of journalism, poetry, stories, essays and novels, to earn sustenance for his soul.

In the time of peace and happiness during Tito's Yugoslavia, Bahtijaragic did not succumb to the challenging temptations of the international metropolis. (He served as governor of *Centrom Privredne banke Sarajevo* , the Bosnian state bank service for Francophone countries, headquartered in Paris.) He could have stayed in this role while remaining out of Yugoslavia, but, during the last Balkan Wars, at the end of the second millennium, he emigrated with his family from Bosnia to Germany, and then in 1994 to Vancouver, in Canada.

He is a member of The Writers' Union of Canada and The British Columbia Federation of Writers.

Rifet never served in any army in his life.

Cover Artist: Bill Hoopes is a Canadian artist. He paints primarily in oils, with some watercolour work. Hoopes uses his art to carry a social message – that we examine our role as users and guardians of this planet in order to accept our responsibility for maintaining and preserving our environment. He lives on Bowen Island, near Vancouver, with his family.